BIBLE 200
Teacher's Guide

M000035297

Author:

Alpha Omega Publications

Editor:

Alan Christopherson, M.S.

Alpha Omega
PUBLICATIONS

804 N. 2nd Ave. E.
Rock Rapids, IA 51246-1759

BIBLE 200

LIFEPAC® Overview

BIBLE SCOPE & SEQUENCE

	Grade 1	Grade 2	Grade 3
UNIT 1	**GOD CREATED ALL THINGS** • God created day and night • God created land and sea • God created plants and animals • God created people	**WHO AM I?** • God made us • God loves me • God helps me • God helped Daniel	**LIVING FOR GOD** • I love and obey God • I praise God • I worship God • I serve God
UNIT 2	**GOD LOVES HIS CHILDREN** • God cared for Shadrach, Meshach, and Abednego • God cared for Joash and Esther • God cares for his children • God's children love him	**THE STORY OF MOSES** • The early life of Moses • Life in Midian • Moses returns to Egypt • Life in the desert	**THE LIFE OF JESUS** • Mary and Joseph • Jesus in the Temple • Jesus teaches and saves • Jesus dies and lives again
UNIT 3	**WE CAN PRAY** • We can ask and thank God • We can pray God's special prayer • God listens to us • We listen to God	**GOD AND YOU** • God is great • God keeps his promises • You should obey God • God rewards his people	**GOD'S PLAN FOR JOSEPH** • The dream of Joseph • Joseph and his brothers • Joseph in Egypt • God watched over Joseph
UNIT 4	**GOD WANTS YOU TO BE GOOD** • Jesus says love God • God says to love others • You show your love • God says to love yourself	**HOW THE BIBLE CAME TO US** • Moses and the Prophets • David and Solomon • The Apostles and Paul • Bible translators	**YOU CAN USE THE BIBLE** • The books of the Bible • How to read and study the Bible • How to find verses • How to memorize verses
UNIT 5	**OLD TESTAMENT STORIES** • Joseph, Elijah, Jonathan, and David • Miriam and Deborah • A rich woman and her son • Ishmael and Mephibosheth	**DAVID'S SLING** • David with the sheep • David and the prophet • David and Saul • David and the giant	**GOD CARES FOR HIS PEOPLE** • God's love for people • God guides people • God protects people • God blesses people
UNIT 6	**GOD'S PROMISE** • God's Old Testament promises • God's promises kept • The birth of the Promised One • The life of the Promised One	**GOD IS EVERYWHERE** • Understanding the beginning • Understanding God • The creation • God's will	**THE BIBLE IS GOD'S WORD** • The writers of God's Word • God's Word is preserved • God's Word changes lives • Promises of God's Word
UNIT 7	**JESUS, OUR SAVIOR** • Jesus taught the people • Jesus healed the people • Jesus saves the people • Jesus will come again	**THE STORY OF JOSEPH** • Joseph as a boy at home • The worship of Joseph • Joseph in Egypt • Joseph and the famine	**ARCHAEOLOGY AND THE BIBLE** • The search for treasure • Clues from old stories • Explaining the puzzles • Joining the search
UNIT 8	**GOD CALLS MISSIONARIES** • The woman at the well • Stephen and Paul • Missionaries today • God calls missionaries	**GOD AND THE FAMILY** • The first family • Abraham's family • Happy families • God's promise to children	**GOD GAVE US THE NEED FOR FRIENDS** • We need love • We need friendship • God commands our love • Love for others
UNIT 9	**NEW TESTAMENT STORIES** • Lazarus, Thomas, Stephen • Mary, Anna, Lydia • Children in the New Testament • Jesus and the children	**GOD MADE THE NATIONS** • The people of Babel • God's judgment at Babel • The new nation • Our big world	**GOD'S PEOPLE HELP OTHERS** • All people are created by God • God loves me • God's love to others • God is my Father
UNIT 10	**GOD GAVE YOU MANY GIFTS** • God created all things • God loves his children • God gave us his Word • God gave us his Son	**GOD, HIS WORD, AND YOU** • God as our Father • The Word of God • Life with God • Belonging to God	**GOD'S WORD, JESUS, AND YOU** • God speaks to Man • Writers of the Word • Jesus and the Word • God's family

BIBLE SCOPE & SEQUENCE

Grade 4	Grade 5	Grade 6	
HOW CAN I LIVE FOR GOD? • Peter found Jesus • Peter fished for men • To be born into God's family • To be fruitful through the Spirit	**HOW OTHERS LIVED FOR GOD** • Fellow-laborers with God • Abraham, a man of faith • Servants of God • Co-workers with God	**FROM CREATION TO MOSES** • Creation • The Flood • Abraham and his descendants • Moses and the Law	UNIT 1
GOD'S KNOWLEDGE • Knowledge to create • Learning God's knowledge • The benefits of God's knowledge • Using God's knowledge	**ANGELS** • Characteristics of Angels • Kinds of Angels • The ministry of Angels • Angels in the life of Jesus	**FROM JOSHUA TO SAMUEL** • Conquest and division of the land • The death of Joshua • The Judges of Israel • Ruth, Naomi, and Boaz	UNIT 2
SAUL BEGINS TO LIVE FOR GOD • Saul persecutes the Christians • God changes Saul • Saul preaches about Jesus • Paul belongs to Christ	**THE PRESENCE OF GOD** • Everywhere as God • Everywhere as a person • In the lives of people • In my life	**THE KINGDOM OF ISRAEL** • Samuel and Saul • The reign of David • The reign of Solomon • The books of poetry	UNIT 3
THE BIBLE AND ME • Reading and learning the Bible • Thinking about the Bible • Memorizing the Bible • Living the Bible way	**BIBLE METHODS AND STRUCTURE** • One book with many parts • Books of history • Books of poetry and prophecy • Books of the New Testament	**THE DIVIDED KINGDOM** • From Jeroboam to Captivity • Prophets of Judah and Israel • From Hezekiah to Captivity • Prophets of remaining kingdom	UNIT 4
GOD CARES FOR US • The Twenty-third Psalm • Jesus and the sheep • David as a shepherd • Daniel as a helper	**THE CHRISTIAN IN THE WORLD** • Instruction and correction • Learning correct behavior • Relationships at school • Relationships in the world	**CAPTIVITY AND RESTORATION** • The prophets of the Captivity • The returns from exile • The prophets of the Restoration • Creation to Restoration	UNIT 5
HOW CAN I KNOW GOD EXISTS • God's plan for the Jews • A Jewish Savior • Man searches for God • Man needs God	**PROVING WHAT WE BELIEVE** • The Bible is God's Word • Evidence from the Bible • Evidence from history and science • Knowing that Christ arose	**THE LIFE OF JESUS** • Birth and background • The first years of ministry • The latter years of ministry • The death and Resurrection	UNIT 6
GEOGRAPHY OF THE OLD TESTAMENT • Bible geography • Description of the land • Abram's nomadic life • Abraham's descendants	**MISSIONARY JOURNEYS OF PAUL** • Paul's background • Paul's missionary journeys • The Jerusalem Council • Paul's last years	**THE FOLLOWERS OF JESUS** • The disciples of Jesus • The friends of Jesus • Miracles of Jesus • The message of Jesus	UNIT 7
GOD-GIVEN WORTH • Who Am I? • God is my Creator • God is my Father • Knowing God's love	**GOD CREATED MAN FOR ETERNITY** • Preparing for eternity • Christ is our Judge • The judgment of the Christian • The judgment of the unsaved	**THE APOSTLE PAUL** • Paul's background and conversion • Paul's missionary journeys • Paul's letters to churches • Paul's letters to people	UNIT 8
WITNESSING FOR JESUS • Loving God and others • Following Jesus • Knowing who Jesus is • Following Paul's example	**AUTHORITY AND LAW** • God is the source of law • The model of law • The authority of the family • Our authority of government	**HEBREWS AND GENERAL EPISTLES** • The book of Hebrews • James and 1st and 2nd Peter • The three Johns • The book of Jude	UNIT 9
GOD'S WAY IS PERFECT • Seeking knowledge • Science & geography • Living God's way • Loving God's way	**ANGELS, THE BIBLE, LIVING FOR GOD** • Presence of God and Angels • Understanding the Bible • Areas of service • The order of authority	**REVELATION AND REVIEW** • The Lord Jesus in Revelation • End-time events • Old Testament review • New Testament review	UNIT 10

BIBLE SCOPE & SEQUENCE

	Grade 7	Grade 8	Grade 9
UNIT 1	WORSHIP • The nature of worship • Old Testament worship • New Testament worship • True worship	PRAYER • Organization of the Lord's Prayer • Purpose of the Lord's Prayer • History of prayer • Practical uses of prayer	THE NEW TESTAMENT • Inter-Testamental period • Pharisees and Sadducees • New Testament themes • New Testament events
UNIT 2	MANKIND • The origin of man • The fall of man • The re-creation of man • The mission of man	SIN AND SALVATION • The nature of sin • The need for salvation • How to receive salvation • The results of salvation	THE GOSPELS • Matthew • Mark • Luke • John
UNIT 3	THE ATTRIBUTES OF GOD • God's nature of love • God's expression of love • The mercy of God • The grace of God	ATTRIBUTES OF GOD • God's justice • God's immutability • God's eternal nature • God's love	THE ACTS OF THE APOSTLES • The writer • The purpose • Pentecost • Missions
UNIT 4	FULFILLED PROPHECIES OF CHRIST • Method of the First Advent • Purpose of the First Advent • Offices of the Messiah foretold • Offices of the Messiah fulfilled	EARLY CHURCH LEADERS • The early church • The church of the Middle Ages • The Renaissance • The Reformation	THE PAULINE EPISTLES • Paul as a person • The early epistles • Prison epistles • The later epistles
UNIT 5	NEW LIFE IN CHRIST • Life before and after Christ • Growing in Christ • Life in the Spirit • The life of grace	EARLY CHURCH HISTORY • The Roman Empire • The background of the Jews • The ministry of Jesus • The Jerusalem church	GENERAL EPISTLES • James • First and Second Peter • First, Second, and Third John • Hebrews and Jude
UNIT 6	THE PSALMS • The history of the Psalms • Types and uses of the Psalms • Hebrew poetry • Study of Psalm 100	THE EARLY CHURCHES • The church at Antioch • The missionary journeys • The Jerusalem Conference • New Testament churches	THE REVELATION OF JESUS CHRIST • The seven churches • The seven seals and trumpets • The seven signs and plagues • The seven judgments and wonders
UNIT 7	THE LIFE OF CHRIST: PART 1 • Early life of Christ • Beginning of Christ's ministry • The early Judean ministry • The early Galilean ministry	THE BOOK OF PROVERBS • Literary forms and outline • Objectives and purposes • Influence on the New Testament • Key themes	JOB AND SUFFERING • The scenes of Job • Attitudes toward suffering • Christ's suffering on Earth • The victory of Christ's suffering
UNIT 8	THE LIFE OF CHRIST: PART 2 • The public ministry in Galilee • The private ministry in Galilee • The Judean ministry • The Perean ministry	TODAY'S PROBLEMS • Guidance for behavior • Characteristics of friendship • Studying effectively • Finding God's will	HOW TO SHARE CHRIST • Personal evangelism • Outreach to others • Personal and family missions • Assisting a missionary
UNIT 9	THE LIFE OF CHRIST: PART 3 • Jesus's final ministry • Jesus's sufferings and crucifixion • Jesus's resurrection and ascension	UNDERSTANDING PARENTS • Human parents • Biblical parents • Children's responsibility • Parents and children as a team	GOD'S WILL FOR MY LIFE • The desire of the heart • The Word and work of God • The importance of goals • The use of talents
UNIT 10	GOD'S PLAN IN CHRIST • God and His plan • Man's history • Jesus Christ fulfills God's plan • Man's response to God	WALKING WITH GOD • Prayer and salvation • The attributes of God • The early church leaders • Christian living	THE WALK WITH CHRIST • Background of the New Testament • The Epistles and Revelation • The importance of suffering • God's will for my life

BIBLE SCOPE & SEQUENCE

Grade 10	Grade 11	Grade 12	
CREATION TO ABRAHAM • The six days of creation • The fall of man • Noah and his descendants • Nations of the earth	**THE FAITHFULNESS OF GOD** • Affirmation of God's faithfulness • Nature of God's faithfulness • Manifestations of God's faithfulness • Implications of God's faithfulness	**KNOWING YOURSELF** • Your creation by God • Interacting with others • A child and servant of God • Your personal skills	UNIT 1
ABRAHAM TO MOSES • Abraham's call and promise • The covenant with Isaac • The life of Jacob • Joseph and his family	**ROMANS: PART 1** • The Roman Empire and Church • The book of Romans • Paul's message to the Romans • Sin and salvation in Romans	**CHRISTIAN MINISTRIES** • Christian ministry defined • Church related ministries • Other ministries • A ministry as a career	UNIT 2
EXODUS AND WANDERINGS • The journey to Sinai • The giving of the Law • Numbering the people • The book of Deuteronomy	**ROMANS: PART 2** • The chosen of God • Service and submission • From sin to salvation • The victory of salvation	**CHOOSING A CHRISTIAN MINISTRY** • Where to look for a ministry • What to look for in a ministry • How to look for a ministry • Choosing a ministry for a career	UNIT 3
ISRAEL IN CANAAN • Preparing for battle • The fight for the land • Dividing the land • The death of Joshua	**THE DOCTRINE OF JESUS CHRIST** • Identity and incarnation of Christ • The individuality of Christ • Christ's work on the Cross • Christ's work after the Cross	**GODHEAD** • Old Testament view • New Testament view • Historical Perspectives • Faith and man's relationship	UNIT 4
THE JUDGES AND SPIRITUAL DECLINE • Background of Judges • History of the Judges • Examples of spiritual decay • Ruth and redemption	**THE NATION OF ISRAEL** • The covenant with Abraham • Israel as a nation • Old Testament archaeology • New Testament archaeology	**ATTRIBUTES OF GOD** • The Holiness of God • The Goodness of God • Holiness and the believer • Goodness and the Creation	UNIT 5
THE KINGDOM • Samuel and Saul • David • Solomon • Hebrew poetry	**HISTORY OF THE CANON** • Revelation and inspiration • Illumination and interpretation • Authority of the Bible • Formation of the Bible	**THE EPISTLES OF JAMES AND JOHN** • James the man • The message of James • John the man • The message of John's epistles	UNIT 6
THE DIVIDED KINGDOM • Jeroboam to Ahab • Ahab to Jehu • Jehu to Assyrian Captivity • Prophets of the period	**FRIENDSHIP, DATING, AND MARRIAGE** • Meaning and role of friendship • Perspectives of dating • Principles of relationships • The structure of marriage	**DANIEL** • A man of conviction • An interpreter of dreams • A watchman in prayer • A man of visions	UNIT 7
THE REMAINING KINGDOM • The time of Hezekiah • Manasseh to Josiah • Jehoahaz to the exile • Prophets of the period	**THE PURSUIT OF HAPPINESS** • Solomon's succession • Solomon's prosperity • Solomon's fall • Solomon's reflection	**COMPARATIVE RELIGIONS** • Elements of Christianity • The validity of Christian faith • World religions • The occult	UNIT 8
THE CAPTIVITY • Prophets of the period • Jeremiah • Ezekiel • Daniel	**ANSWERS FOR AGNOSTICS** • Integrity of the Bible • Doctrines of the Bible • Interpretation of the Bible • Application of the Bible	**WISDOM FOR TODAY'S YOUTH** • Life and character of David • Life and riches of Solomon • Psalms and Proverbs • The Bible and literature	UNIT 9
THE RESTORATION • First return from exile • The Jews preserved • Second return from exile • Haggai, Zechariah, and Malachi	**GOD, HIS WORD, AND THE CHRISTIAN** • The uniqueness of the Bible • History of Israel • God revealed in the Bible • Principles for living	**THE CHRISTIAN** • Christian fundamentals • Growing in Christian maturity • A ministry for Christ • A testimony for Christ	UNIT 10

STRUCTURE OF THE LIFEPAC CURRICULUM

The LIFEPAC curriculum is conveniently structured to provide one teacher's guide containing teacher support material with answer keys and ten student worktexts for each subject at grade levels 2 through 12. The worktext format of the LIFEPACs allows the student to read the textual information and complete workbook activities all in the same booklet. The easy-to-follow LIFEPAC numbering system lists the grade as the first number(s) and the last two digits as the number of the series. For example, the Language Arts LIFEPAC at the 6th grade level, 5th book in the series would be LAN0605.

Each LIFEPAC is divided into three to five sections and begins with an introduction or overview of the booklet as well as a series of specific learning objectives to give a purpose to the study of the LIFEPAC. The introduction and objectives are followed by a vocabulary section which may be found at the beginning of each section at the lower levels or in the glossary at the high school level. Vocabulary words are used to develop word recognition and should not be confused with the spelling words introduced later in the LIFEPAC. The student should learn all vocabulary words before working the LIFEPAC sections to improve comprehension, retention, and reading skills.

Each activity or written assignment in grades 2 through 12 has a number for easy identification, such as 1.1. The first number corresponds to the LIFEPAC section and the number to the right of the decimal is the number of the activity.

Teacher checkpoints, which are essential to maintain quality learning, are found at various locations throughout the LIFEPAC. The teacher should check 1) neatness of work and penmanship, 2) quality of understanding (tested with a short oral quiz), 3) thoroughness of answers (complete sentences and paragraphs, correct spelling, etc.), 4) completion of activities (no blank spaces), and 5) accuracy of answers as compared to the answer key (all answers correct).

The self test questions in grades 2 through 12 are also number coded for easy reference. For example, 2.015 means that this is the 15th question in the self test of Section 2. The first number corresponds to the LIFEPAC section, the zero indicates that it is a self test question, and the number to the right of the zero the question number.

The LIFEPAC test is packaged at the center of each LIFEPAC. It should be removed and put aside before giving the booklet to the student for study.

Answer and test keys in grades 2 through 12 have the same numbering system as the LIFEPACs. The student may be given access to the answer keys (not the test keys) under teacher supervision so that they can score their own work.

A thorough study of the Scope & Sequence by the teacher before instruction begins is essential to the success of the student. The teacher should become familiar with expected skill mastery and understand how these grade-level skills fit into the overall skill development of the curriculum. The teacher should also preview the objectives that appear at the beginning of each LIFEPAC for additional preparation and planning.

TEST SCORING AND GRADING

Answer keys and test keys give examples of correct answers. They convey the idea, but the student may use many ways to express a correct answer. The teacher should check for the essence of the answer, not for the exact wording. Many questions are high level and require thinking and creativity on the part of the student. Each answer should be scored based on whether or not the main idea written by the student matches the model example. "Any Order" or "Either Order" in a key indicates that no particular order is necessary to be correct.

Most self tests and LIFEPAC tests at the lower elementary levels are scored at 1 point per answer; however, the upper levels may have a point system awarding 2 to 5 points for various answers or questions. Further, the total test points will vary; they may not always equal 100 points. They may be 78, 85, 100, 105, etc.

Example 1

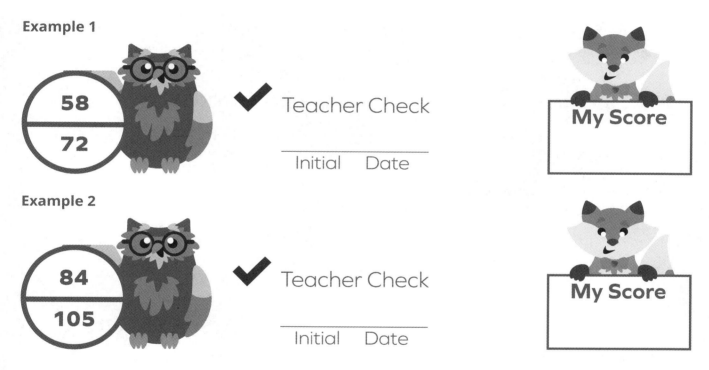

Example 2

A score box similar to ex. 1 above is located at the end of each self test and on the front of the LIFEPAC test. The bottom score, 72, represents the total number of points possible on the test. The upper score, 58, represents the number of points your student will need to receive an 80% or passing grade. If you wish to establish the exact percentage that your student has achieved, find the total points of their correct answers and divide it by the bottom number (in this case 72). For example, if your student has a point total of 65, divide 65 by 72 for a grade of 90%. Referring to ex. 2, on a test with a total of 105 possible points, the student would have to receive a minimum of 84 correct points for an 80% or passing grade. If your student has received 93 points, simply divide the 93 by 105 for a percentage grade of 89%. Students who receive a score below 80% should review the LIFEPAC and retest using the appropriate Alternate Test found in the Teacher's Guide.

The following is a guideline to assign letter grades for completed LIFEPACs based on a maximum total score of 100 points.

Example:

LIFEPAC Test	=	60% of the Total Score (or percent grade)
Self Test	=	25% of the Total Score (average percent of self tests)
Reports	=	10% or 10* points per LIFEPAC
Oral Work	=	5% or 5* points per LIFEPAC

*Determined by the teacher's subjective evaluation of the student's daily work.

Example:

LIFEPAC Test Score	= 92%	92 × .60	=	55 points
Self Test Average	= 90%	90 × .25	=	23 points
Reports			=	8 points
Oral Work			=	4 points
TOTAL POINTS			=	90 points

Grade Scale based on point system:

100 – 94	=	A
93 – 86	=	B
85 – 77	=	C
76 – 70	=	D
Below 70	=	F

TEACHER HINTS AND STUDYING TECHNIQUES

LIFEPAC activities are written to check the level of understanding of the preceding text. The student may look back to the text as necessary to complete these activities; however, a student should never attempt to do the activities without reading (studying) the text first. Self tests and LIFEPAC tests are never open book tests.

Language arts activities (skill integration) often appear within other subject curriculum. The purpose is to give the student an opportunity to test his skill mastery outside of the context in which it was presented.

Writing complete answers (paragraphs) to some questions is an integral part of the LIFEPAC curriculum in all subjects. This builds communication and organization skills, increases understanding and retention of ideas, and helps enforce good penmanship. Complete sentences should be encouraged for this type of activity. Obviously, single words or phrases do not meet the intent of the activity, since multiple lines are given for the response.

Review is essential to student success. Time invested in review where review is suggested will be time saved in correcting errors later. Self tests, unlike the section activities, are closed book. This procedure helps to identify weaknesses before they become too great to overcome. Certain objectives from self tests are cumulative and test previous sections; therefore, good preparation for a self test must include all material studied up to that testing point.

The following procedure checklist has been found to be successful in developing good study habits in the LIFEPAC curriculum.

1. Read the introduction and Table of Contents.
2. Read the objectives.
3. Recite and study the entire vocabulary (glossary) list.
4. Study each section as follows:
   a. Read the introduction and study the section objectives.
   b. Read all the text for the entire section, but answer none of the activities.
   c. Return to the beginning of the section and memorize each vocabulary word and definition.
   d. Reread the section, complete the activities, check the answers with the answer key, correct all errors, and have the teacher check.
   e. Read the self test but do not answer the questions.
   f. Go to the beginning of the first section and reread the text and answers to the activities up to the self test you have not yet done.
   g. Answer the questions to the self test without looking back.
   h. Have the self test checked by the teacher.
   i. Correct the self test and have the teacher check the corrections.
   j. Repeat steps a–i for each section.
5. Use the **SQ3R** method to prepare for the LIFEPAC test.
   Scan the whole LIFEPAC.
   Question yourself on the objectives.
   Read the whole LIFEPAC again.
   Recite through an oral examination.
   Review weak areas.
6. Take the LIFEPAC test as a closed book test.
7. LIFEPAC tests are administered and scored under direct teacher supervision. Students who receive scores below 80% should review the LIFEPAC using the **SQ3R** study method and take the Alternate Test located in the Teacher's Guide. The final test grade may be the grade on the Alternate Test or an average of the grades from the original LIFEPAC test and the Alternate Test.

GOAL SETTING AND SCHEDULES

Each school must develop its own schedule, because no single set of procedures will fit every situation. The following is an example of a daily schedule that includes the five LIFEPAC subjects as well as time slotted for special activities.

Possible Daily Schedule

8:15 – 8:25	Pledges, prayer, songs, devotions, etc.
8:25 – 9:10	Bible
9:10 – 9:55	Language Arts
9:55 – 10:15	Recess (juice break)
10:15 – 11:00	Math
11:00 – 11:45	History & Geography
11:45 – 12:30	Lunch, recess, quiet time
12:30 – 1:15	Science
1:15 –	Drill, remedial work, enrichment*

***Enrichment:** Computer time, physical education, field trips, fun reading, games and puzzles, family business, hobbies, resource persons, guests, crafts, creative work, electives, music appreciation, projects.*

Basically, two factors need to be considered when assigning work to a student in the LIFEPAC curriculum.

The first is time. An average of 45 minutes should be devoted to each subject, each day. Remember, this is only an average. Because of extenuating circumstances, a student may spend only 15 minutes on a subject one day and the next day spend 90 minutes on the same subject.

The second factor is the number of pages to be worked in each subject. A single LIFEPAC is designed to take three to four weeks to complete. Allowing about three to four days for LIFEPAC introduction, review, and tests, the student has approximately 15 days to complete the LIFEPAC pages. Simply take the number of pages in the LIFEPAC, divide it by 15 and you will have the number of pages that must be completed on a daily basis to keep the student on schedule. For example, a LIFEPAC containing 45 pages will require three completed pages per day. Again, this is only an average. While working a 45-page LIFEPAC, the student may complete only one page the first day if the text has a lot of activities or reports, but go on to complete five pages the next day.

Long-range planning requires some organization. Because the traditional school year originates in the early fall of one year and continues to late spring of the following year, a calendar should be devised that covers this period of time. Approximate beginning and completion dates can be noted on the calendar as well as special occasions such as holidays, vacations and birthdays. Since each LIFEPAC takes three to four weeks or 18 days to complete, it should take about 180 school days to finish a set of ten LIFEPACs. Starting at the beginning school date, mark off 18 school days on the calendar and that will become the targeted completion date for the first LIFEPAC. Continue marking the calendar until you have established dates for the remaining nine LIFEPACs making adjustments for previously noted holidays and vacations. If all five subjects are being used, the ten established target dates should be the same for the LIFEPACs in each subject.

TEACHING SUPPLEMENTS

The sample weekly lesson plan and student grading sheet forms are included in this section as teacher support materials and may be duplicated at the convenience of the teacher.

The student grading sheet is provided for those who desire to follow the suggested guidelines for assignment of letter grades as previously discussed. The student's self test scores should be posted as percentage grades. When the LIFEPAC is completed, the teacher should average the self test grades, multiply the average by .25, and post the points in the box marked self test points. The LIFEPAC percentage grade should be multiplied by .60 and posted. Next, the teacher should award and post points for written reports and oral work. A report may be any type of written work assigned to the student whether it is a LIFEPAC or additional learning activity. Oral work includes the student's ability to respond orally to questions which may or may not be related to LIFEPAC activities or any type of oral report assigned by the teacher. The points may then be totaled and a final grade entered along with the date that the LIFEPAC was completed.

The Student Record Book which was specifically designed for use with the Alpha Omega curriculum provides space to record weekly progress for one student over a nine-week period as well as a place to post self test and LIFEPAC scores. The Student Record Books are available through the current Alpha Omega catalog; however, unlike the enclosed forms these books are not for duplication and should be purchased in sets of four to cover a full academic year.

WEEKLY LESSON PLANNER

Week of:

	Subject	Subject	Subject	Subject
Monday				
Tuesday	Subject	Subject	Subject	Subject
Wednesday	Subject	Subject	Subject	Subject
Thursday	Subject	Subject	Subject	Subject
Friday	Subject	Subject	Subject	Subject

WEEKLY LESSON PLANNER

Week of:

	Subject	Subject	Subject	Subject
Monday				
Tuesday	Subject	Subject	Subject	Subject
Wednesday	Subject	Subject	Subject	Subject
Thursday	Subject	Subject	Subject	Subject
Friday	Subject	Subject	Subject	Subject

Student Name _____   Year _____

Bible

LP	Self Test Scores by Sections					Self Test Points	LIFEPAC Test	Oral Points	Report Points	Final Grade	Date
	1	2	3	4	5						
01											
02											
03											
04											
05											
06											
07											
08											
09											
10											

History & Geography

LP	Self Test Scores by Sections					Self Test Points	LIFEPAC Test	Oral Points	Report Points	Final Grade	Date
	1	2	3	4	5						
01											
02											
03											
04											
05											
06											
07											
08											
09											
10											

Language Arts

LP	Self Test Scores by Sections					Self Test Points	LIFEPAC Test	Oral Points	Report Points	Final Grade	Date
	1	2	3	4	5						
01											
02											
03											
04											
05											
06											
07											
08											
09											
10											

Student Name _____   Year _____

Math

| LP | Self Test Scores by Sections | | | | | Self Test Points | LIFEPAC Test | Oral Points | Report Points | Final Grade | Date |
	1	2	3	4	5						
01											
02											
03											
04											
05											
06											
07											
08											
09											
10											

Science

| LP | Self Test Scores by Sections | | | | | Self Test Points | LIFEPAC Test | Oral Points | Report Points | Final Grade | Date |
	1	2	3	4	5						
01											
02											
03											
04											
05											
06											
07											
08											
09											
10											

Spelling/Electives

| LP | Self Test Scores by Sections | | | | | Self Test Points | LIFEPAC Test | Oral Points | Report Points | Final Grade | Date |
	1	2	3	4	5						
01											
02											
03											
04											
05											
06											
07											
08											
09											
10											

INSTRUCTIONS FOR BIBLE

The Alpha Omega Curriculum from grades 2 through 12 was written with the daily instructional material written directly in the LIFEPACs. The student is encouraged to read and follow his own instructional material thus developing independent study habits. The teacher should introduce the LIFEPAC to the student, set a required completion schedule, complete teacher checks, be available for questions regarding both subject content and procedures, administer and grade tests and develop additional learning activities as desired. Teachers working with several students may schedule their time so that students are assigned to a quiet work activity when it is necessary to spend instructional time with one particular student.

The Teacher Notes section of the Teacher's Guide lists the required or suggested materials for the LIFEPACs and provides additional learning activities for the students. The materials section refers only to LIFEPAC materials and does not include materials which may be needed for the additional activities. Additional learning activities provide a change from the daily school routine, encourage the student's interest in learning and may be used as a reward for good study habits.

BIBLE 201

Unit 1: Who Am I?

TEACHER NOTES

MATERIALS NEEDED FOR LIFEPAC	
Required	Suggested
(None)	• Bible storybook • Bible dictionary • Bible commentary • Bible map • teaching pictures of the life of Daniel

ADDITIONAL LEARNING ACTIVITIES

Section 1 - God Made Us

1. Discuss the relative concept of size. Have students question their sizes in relationship to animals, buildings, parents, friends, and God.

2. Discuss the limitations of childhood. Name some activities children cannot do as well as adults. Name some special activities for children. The child *is* special.

3. Discuss articles and concepts that a person may or may not outgrow. Discuss the truth that we never outgrow the love of God.

4. Draw pictures of families representing size and structure. Compare the drawings with other students.

5. Study your face in a mirror. How do you see yourself? How do your friends see you?

Section 2 - God Loves Me

1. Discuss heaven, the wonderful place God has prepared for those who love Him.

2. Discuss who and what will be in heaven. Who will not be in heaven?

3. Discuss the concept of death with the class.

4. Make a large mural of what you think heaven will be like. Include people you would expect to see.

5. Students may construct a scroll using brown paper and copy a favorite Bible verse on the scroll.

Section 3 - God Helps Me

1. Discuss these questions with your class.

    a. How can we be helpful to others?

    b. How can you help God?

    c. What special work can you do now?

2. Visit a rest home and share songs, poems, and Bible recitation with the residents.

3. Draw pictures illustrating how you were helpful to others during the week.

4. Think of a helpful project to do tonight in your home.

Section 4 - God Helped Daniel

1. Discuss dreams and their importance to restful sleep.

2. Research dreams in a children's encyclopedia or online.

3. Discuss how we can honor God by what we eat. Emphasize the care of our bodies.

4. Discuss the importance of prayer in Daniel's life, and in our lives.

5. Discuss whether Daniel would have had an effective testimony if he had complained about his situation.

6. On a Bible map, locate Israel and Babylon.

7. Research the law of the Medes and Persians (Esther 1:19 and 8:8).

8. Look in the book of Daniel. Find Daniel's other name.

9. From the letters in the name *King Nebuchadnezzar*, make as many words as you can (examples: head, buzz, red).

Administer the LIFEPAC Test.

The test is to be administered in one session. Give no help except with directions.
Evaluate the tests and review areas where the students have done poorly.
Review the pages and activities that stress the concepts tested.
If necessary, administer the Alternate LIFEPAC Test.

ANSWER KEYS

SECTION 1

1.1	I am
1.2	God
1.3	Yes
1.4	I will praise Thee
1.5	Yes
1.6	Yes
1.7	Jesus
1.8	for I am fearfully and wonderfully made
1.9	Teacher check
1.10	Bible
1.11	special
1.12	God
1.13	praise, wonderfully

SELF TEST 1

1.01	hair
1.02	slow
1.03	family
1.04	special
1.05	me
1.06	I will, I am, made
1.07	yes
1.08	yes
1.09	no
1.010	yes
1.011	yes
1.012	Jesus
1.013	special
1.014	God's
1.015	family
1.016	heavenly

SECTION 2

2.1	loves me, sent Jesus
2.2	need Jesus, can feel sad
2.3	Jesus was sent to save us
2.4	Teacher check
2.5	lived
2.6	stories
2.7	said
2.8	teach, save
2.9	save, help, teach
2.10	lost, help, stop
2.11	save, help, teach
2.12	Teacher check
2.13	God
2.14	Jesus
2.15	Jesus
2.16	Jesus
2.17	whosoever, perish, life
2.18	1. Bible
	2. people
	3. forever
	4. God
	5. love
	6. Jesus

SELF TEST 2

2.01	God, gave, Son, Him, life
2.02	yes
2.03	no
2.04	yes
2.05	yes
2.06	yes
2.07	yes
2.08	yes
2.09	yes
2.010	no
2.011	yes
2.012	God
2.013	Jesus
2.014	Bible
2.015	people
2.016	love
2.017	forever
2.018	save, teach, help
2.019	Lord, Savior

SECTION 3

3.1	Teacher check
3.2	Teacher check
3.3	helpful
3.4	kind
3.5	honest
3.6	Obey
3.7	loving
3.8	kind
3.9	obey
3.10	empty trash
3.11	love others
3.12	pick up toys
3.13	fill up tub
3.14	use nice words
3.15	look after baby
3.16	helpful
3.17	can
3.18	must
3.19	will
3.20	should
3.21	must
3.22	My work is to let people see the love of Jesus in me.
3.23	everyone
3.24	forgive
3.25	Jesus
3.26	God

SELF TEST 3

3.01	ye, word, deed, Jesus, thanks
3.02	begotten
3.03	love
3.04	recite
3.05	sin
3.06	praise
3.07	yes
3.08	yes
3.09	yes
3.010	yes
3.011	yes
3.012	save, help, teach
3.013	loving, kind, honest
3.014	love
3.015	ask
3.016	forgive

SECTION 4

4.1	God's Word	4.20	told	-	fold
4.2	Israel		fight	-	might
4.3	strong		king	-	ring
4.4	smart		fell	-	well
4.5	Teacher check		mad	-	dad
4.6	King Nebuchadnezzar		dream	-	cream
4.7	Daniel and his three friends	4.21	blessed
4.8	palace	4.22	tricked
4.9	to obey god	4.23	knew about
4.10	after ten days	4.24	sorry
4.11	able to learn, be very smart, know the meaning of dreams	4.25	faith
		4.26	true
4.12	gave me a family	4.27	obeyed
	gave me friends	4.28	blessed
	gave me a healthy body	4.29	protected
	made me able to learn	4.30	obey, bless, protect
	gave me a happy heart	4.31	lēaders
	gave me a good school	4.32	rūlε
4.13	Teacher check	4.33	līkε
4.14	God	4.34	prōtect
4.15	Blessed	4.35	rēad
4.16	forever	4.36	mākε
4.17	wisdom and might	4.37	nāmε
4.18	Teacher check	4.38	wrītε
4.19	2, 4, 1, 3	4.39	rule
		4.40	like
		4.41	make
		4.42	name
		4.43	write

SELF TEST 4

4.01 Blessed, God, wisdom, might
4.02 yes
4.03 yes
4.04 yes
4.05 yes
4.06 no
4.07 Son
4.08 Israelite
4.09 child
4.010 Bible
4.011 Blessed
4.012 sinned
4.013 love
4.014 Jesus
4.015 God
4.016 made
4.017 protect
4.018 blessed
4.019 kill
4.020 happy
4.021 true
4.022 a great ruler
a strong body
understand dreams
to be very smart

LIFEPAC TEST

1. ruler
2. recite
3. everlasting
4. protect
5. Jesus
6. God, loved, He, Son, Him, have, life
7. yes
8. yes
9. no
10. no
11. yes
12. I will, I am, made
13. a. yes
    b. yes
    c. yes
14. ye, word, all, name, Jesus
15. God sent Jesus to save me.
16. Daniel, name, God, ever, His

ALTERNATE LIFEPAC TEST

1. love
2. different
3. praise
4. begotten
5. believe
6. die
7. ruler
8. country
9. no
10. yes
11. no
12. yes
13. no
14. no
15. Example: I am special because God made me and He loves me.
16. loved, world, gave, son, whosoever perish, life

BIBLE 201

ALTERNATE LIFEPAC TEST

Name _____

Date _____

My Score

18
22

Each answer = 1 point

Write the correct word from the box on each line.

praise	different	love	begotten	made	believe

1. I am special because of God's _____ .

2. God made everybody to be _____ .

3. We should _____ God because we are fearfully and wonderfully made.

4. Jesus is God's only _____ son.

5. To be a member of God's family I must _____ in Jesus.

Circle the correct word.

6.   perish

      die   sing   praise

7.   Nebuchadnezzar

      ruler   city   food

8.   Babylon

      king   helper   country

Circle *Yes* or *No*.

9.   King Darius shut the lion's mouth.

      Yes   No

10.   Daniel was protected by God.

      Yes   No

11.   Daniel killed the lions.

      Yes   No

12.   Daniel had faith that God would protect him.

      Yes   No

13.   King Darius was sad when Daniel was saved from the lions.

      Yes   No

14.   Daniel was safe from the lions because he ate his vegetables.

      Yes   No

Write a sentence telling why you are special.

15. _____

_____

_____

Write the missing word on each line.

16. "For God so _____ the _____ ,

that He _____ His only begotten

_____ , that _____

believeth in Him should not _____ ,

but have everlasting _____ ."

John 3:16

BIBLE 202

Unit 2: The Story of Moses

TEACHER NOTES

MATERIALS NEEDED FOR LIFEPAC	
Required	Suggested
• Bible	• Bible map • Books about the Holy Land

ADDITIONAL LEARNING ACTIVITIES

Section 1 - Moses' Early Life

1. Discuss how the Hebrews came to be in Egypt. Review the life of Joseph.

2. Locate Egypt on a Bible map. Compare the location of Egypt to the place of Joseph's birth. How did Joseph get to Egypt?

3. Discuss why the king wanted the Hebrew boy babies killed.

4. Invite a basket maker to demonstrate to the class how a basket is made. If possible, perhaps the students could make a simple basket.

5. Show pictures of the pyramids and the Sphinx. Students may wish to bring books with pictures.

6. Discuss the construction of the pyramids, Sphinx, and other ancient Egyptian buildings. Point out that they were built using simple machines.

7. Discuss why Moses had to leave the palace and go to the desert.

Section 2 - Life in Midian

1. Discuss these questions with your class.

   a. How did God talk to Moses? How does He talk with us today?

   b. Did Moses have a Bible?

   c. Why did Moses not want to do as God asked?

   d. What excuses do people give today for not seeking God?

2. Provide pictures of various types of fires. Discuss what happens when fire burns.

3. Read about fire in a children's reference book. Report to the class.

4. Have the children tell or write about how they would have reacted if God had spoken to them in a burning bush.

Section 3 - Moses Returns to Egypt

1. Discuss these questions with your class.

    a. What kind of man was Pharaoh?

    b. What did God do to change Pharaoh's mind?

    c. Which sea did the Hebrews have to cross to escape from Pharaoh's army.

    d. Why do you think Pharaoh changed his mind and went after the Hebrews?

2. Locate the Red Sea on a map of Egypt.

3. Use narration to tell the story of the ten plagues. Allow one student to describe in his/her own words what happened with one of the plagues. Continue until the story of all 10 plagues has been told.

Section 4 - Life in the Desert

1. Discuss the various deserts and their characteristics. Provide reference books on the Arabian desert. Compare the Arabian desert to the Sahara or the American (Sonoran) desert.

2. Have students bring items from the desert for display.

3. Using pictures, sticks, sand, rocks, and other items, make a desert montage.

4. Have students choose a scene or event from Moses' life to illustrate by drawing. Arrange pictures in sequence to form a mural of Moses' life.

5. Discuss the Ten Commandments to ensure the students' understanding of them.

6. Discuss God's provision for the Hebrews and how He provides for us today.

7. View an age-appropriate video on the life of Moses. Is it Biblically accurate? Why or why not?

Administer the LIFEPAC Test.

The test is to be administered in one session. Give no help except with directions.
Evaluate the tests and review areas where the students have done poorly.
Review the pages and activities that stress the concepts tested.
If necessary, administer the Alternate LIFEPAC Test.

ANSWER KEYS

SECTION 1

1.1 Teacher check
1.2 yes
1.3 D
1.4 B
1.5 E
1.6 A
1.7 C
1.8 Pharaoh
1.9 Jochebed
1.10 Pharaoh's daughter
1.11

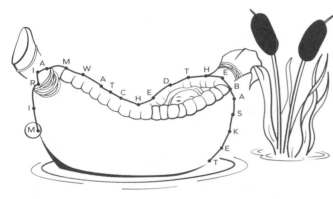

1.12 basket
1.13 **PH**aroah
1.14 **CH**ain
1.15 **SH**eep
1.16 **TH**orn
1.17 5
1.18 7
1.19 2
1.20 3
1.21 6

SELF TEST 1

1.01 from the soldiers
1.02 named Aaron
1.03 basket from tall grass
1.04 for me.
1.05 came to the river for a bath.
1.06 hid
1.07 went
1.08 lived
1.09 ruler
1.010 pick
1.011 did not
1.012 kept
1.013 get
1.014 Jochebed
1.015 help
1.016 take care of Moses
1.017 "Why are you hitting another Hebrew?"
1.018 he ran away from Egypt
1.019 help the people
1.020 help them

SECTION 2

2.1-2.2 Teacher check
2.3 bulrushes
2.4 Egypt
2.5 slaves
2.6 desert
2.7 priest
2.8 sad
2.9 plan
2.10 sheep
2.11 bush
2.12 worship
2.13

Teacher check
2.14 Moses finds a new home.

SELF TEST 2

2.01 no
2.02 yes
2.03 no
2.04 yes
2.05 yes
2.06 no
2.07 d
2.08 c
2.09 a
2.010 e
2.011 b
2.012 desert
2.013 sheep
2.014 wife
2.015 Mount Horeb
2.016 Moses
2.017 plan
2.018 s**heep** c**hain** w**ell** th**orn**

SECTION 3

3.1   no
3.2   yes
3.3   yes
3.4   no
3.5   ACROSS:
    1. miracles
    2. proud
    3. Moses

    DOWN:
    4. go
    5. trouble
    6. straw
    Teacher check
3.6   a. 4
    b. 1
    c.
    d. 5
    e. 3
    f. 2
3.7-3.8 Teacher check
3.9   tenth plague
3.10 Passover
3.11 Egyptians
3.12 blood on doorposts
3.13 Red Sea
3.14 army
3.15 Lord
3.16 Red Sea
3.17 water

SELF TEST 3

3.01   no
3.02   yes
3.03   no
3.04   yes
3.05   no
3.06   Aaron
3.07   miracles
3.08   go
3.09   straw
3.010 Lord
3.011 tenth plague
3.012 Passover
3.013 Egyptians
3.014 blood on doorposts
3.015 Red Sea
3.016 3
3.017 1
3.018 2
3.019 4
3.020 5

SECTION 4

4.1	b
4.2	b
4.3	c
4.4	c
4.5	a
4.6	no
4.7	yes
4.8	no
4.9	yes
4.10	Teacher check

4.11   a. 2   b. 1   c. 1
        d. 1   e. 3   f. 4

SELF TEST 4

4.01	Mount Horeb
4.02	a place to worship God
4.03	a bad taste
4.04	bread from heaven
4.05	a bird eaten as food
4.06	no
4.07	no
4.08	yes
4.09	yes
4.010	no
4.011	no
4.012	The Promised Land
4.013	loves
4.014	went from place to place
4.015	a branch
4.016	cloud

LIFEPAC TEST

1. yes
2. yes
3. no
4. yes
5. yes
6. no
7. yes
8. no
9. yes
10. yes
11. take care of Moses
12. "Why are you hitting another Hebrew?"
13. he ran away from Egypt
14. sheep
15. wife
16. go
17. Lord
18. 5
19. 1
20. 6
21. 3
22. 4
23. 2
24. 7
25. snake
26. water
27. tenth plague
28. blood
29. straw
30. The Ten Commandments
    How to build the Tabernacle
31. Went up a high mountain to see the Promised Land.
    Made Joshua the leader of the Hebrews.

ALTERNATE LIFEPAC TEST

1. c
2. g
3. j
4. a
5. d
6. i
7. f
8. h
9. e
10. b
11. a
12. c
13. c
14. b
15. a
16. c
17. b
18. c
19. yes
20. yes
21. no
22. yes
23. no
24. 1
    4
    5
    3
    2
25. Warts
    Earthquake

BIBLE 202

ALTERNATE LIFEPAC TEST

Name _____

Date _____

My Score

24
30

Each answer = 1 point

Choose the best ending for the sentence. Write the letter for the correct answer on the line.

1. _____ Moses' family hid him

2. _____ The princess

3. _____ Moses wanted to

4. _____ Moses fled

5. _____ The seven sisters

6. _____ God spoke to Moses

7. _____ God did miracles

8. _____ God said to Pharaoh,

9. _____ The Tabernacle was

10. _____ The Ten Commandments were

a. to the desert.

b. written on stone tablets

c. from the soldiers.

d. lived in Midian.

e. a place to worship.

f. through Moses.

g. kept the baby.

h. "Let my people go."

i. from a burning bush.

j. help the people.

Circle the letter for the correct answer.

11. _____ put her baby boy in a basket to save him.

    a. Jochebed

    b. Miriam

    c. Pharaoh's daughter

12. Pharaoh _____ want the Hebrew people to leave Egypt.

    a. did

    b. hid

    c. did not

13. God's plan for the Hebrews was _____ .

    a. to let them be slaves

    b. to ignore them

    c. to help them

14. Moses took care of Jethro's _____ .

    a. goats

    b. sheep

    c. pigs

15. Moses saw the burning bush on _____ .

    a. Mt. Horeb

    b. Mt. Everest

    c. Mt. Fish

16. God wanted _____ to bring the Hebrews out of Egypt.

    a. Amram

    b. Jethro

    c. Moses

17. After leaving slavery, the Hebrews camped near the

_____ .

a. desert

b. Res Sea

c. Egyptians

18. Pharaoh and his _____ went after the Hebrews.

a. wife

b. dogs

c. army

Answer _yes_ or _no_.

19. _____ A priest is one who ministers before God.

20. _____ Moses helped the seven sisters at the well.

21. _____ Pharaoh was nice to the Hebrews.

22. _____ Moses threw soot into the air, and boils came upon the Egyptians.

23. _____ The Hebrews lived in the desert for 20 years.

Number the events in the correct order.

24. _____ Moses was hidden in a basket.

_____ Moses' staff turned into a snake.

_____ God gave Moses the Ten Commandments.

_____ Moses met God in a burning bush.

_____ Moses lived in a palace.

Circle the items that were NOT part of the plagues God sent on the Egyptians.

25.

Water turned to blood	Frogs
Flies	Animals died
Gnats	Darkness
Warts	Boils
Fiery hail	Earthquake
Locusts	Death of the firstborn

BIBLE 203

Unit 3: God and You

TEACHER NOTES

MATERIALS NEEDED FOR LIFEPAC	
Required	Suggested
(None)	• Bible • Bible map

ADDITIONAL LEARNING ACTIVITIES

Section 1 - God Is Great

1. Discuss the greatness of God and the various manifestations of this power.
2. Discuss the implications of the promise made to Abraham.
3. Begin work on a diorama of the life of Abraham.
4. Think of promises for you in the Bible.
5. List all the promises God gave to Abraham.

Section 2 - God Is Dependable

1. Discuss these questions with your class.
   a. What does it mean to be dependable?
   b. What is a miracle?
   c. Would it have been hard for you, if you were Abraham, to leave Ur?
   d. How would you know where to travel?
2. In a book giving the meanings of names, find your name and those of your friends.
3. Make a list of ways you and your family depend on God.

Section 3 - You Should Obey God

1. Tell of a time when you obeyed God even though it was hard to do.
2. Dramatize the journey of Abraham, Isaac, and the servants; the building of the altar; and other important scenes.
3. Locate Mount Moriah on a map of Bible lands.
4. Make a shield from lightweight cardboard. Write on the shield some of the things from which God protects you.

Section 4 - God Rewards His People

1. Discuss why Abraham carried hot coals up the mountain.
2. Discuss the importance of *immediate* obedience. What could have happened if Abraham had said to God as he was about to sacrifice Isaac, "Just a minute. Let me finish what I am doing."?
3. Discuss difficulties a person could encounter by not obeying God.
4. Look up the word *sacrifice* in a Bible dictionary and read about the procedure God's people went through in sacrificing as God specified.

ANSWER KEYS

SECTION 1

1.1 Teacher check
1.2 everything
1.3 hens   -   eggs
trees   -   boats
water   -   drinks
sheep   -   coats
cows   -   milk
1.4 trees, sheep
1.5 coats, boats
1.6 God loves   -   everyone
God has all   -   power
God can do   -   anything
1.7 everything
1.8 no
1.9 yes
1.10 all
1.11 Teacher check
1.12 pl   -   ease
sm   -   ile
gl   -   ad
sh   -   eep
pr   -   etty
1.13 plan, press
small, short
1.14 no
1.15 yes
1.16 yes
1.17 power
1.18 everything
1.19 everywhere
1.20 Abram's wife was   - Sarai
God's chosen people   - Israelites
God promised Abram   - son
Abram obeyed God   - moved to a new land
God gave Abram the   - land as a promise

SELF TEST 1

1.01 best
1.02 anything
1.03 nothing
1.04 all
1.05 nothing
1.06 God, all His works, world
1.07 heaven, everywhere, here
1.08 yes
1.09 yes
1.010 yes
1.011 yes
1.012 no
1.013 man
1.014 God
1.015 wife
1.016 Israelites
1.017 son

SECTION 2

2.1	God is love.
2.2	never
2.3	always
2.4	always
2.5	never
2.6	God
2.7	Abram
2.8	not believing
2.9	depend on
2.10	great praise
2.11	believing God
2.12	I can talk to God.
2.13	I can read God's Word.
2.14	I can trust God
2.15	I can wait for God.
2.16	making
2.17	taking
2.18	having
2.19	giving
2.20	praise
2.21	live
2.22	name
2.23	staggered, God, unbelief, faith, glory
2.24	Abraham
2.25	Sarah
2.26	laughter
2.27	father of nations
2.28	princess
2.29	promise

SELF TEST 2

2.01	not, God, but, giving, God
2.02	yes
2.03	yes
2.04	yes
2.05	yes
2.06	yes
2.07	Make a wish.
2.08	Trust in God
2.09	Do your best.
2.010	Read God's Word
2.011	Talk to God.
2.012	powerful
2.013	rejoice
2.014	glory
2.015	dependable
2.016	promise
2.017	a son
2.018	to a new land
2.019	father of nations
2.020	Isaac
2.021	years
2.022	God
2.023	wait on

SECTION 3

3.1	best
3.2	everywhere
3.3	power
3.4	thanks
3.5	the LORD
3.6	our help and our shield
3.7	yes
3.8	protects
3.9	trust
3.10	believe
3.11	wait
3.12	altar
3.13	sacrifice
3.14	Jesus
3.15	provide
3.16	sins
3.17	no
3.18	yes
3.19	yes
3.20	yes
3.21	yes

SELF TEST 3

3.01	waiteth, Lord, he, help, Psalm
3.02	trust
3.03	believe
3.04	wait
3.05	best
3.06	everywhere
3.07	obey
3.08	God
3.09	nation
3.010	staggered, promise, unbelief, faith, God
3.011	Answers will vary
3.012	Answers will vary
3.013	loved and obeyed Him
3.014	Jesus
3.015	God

SECTION 4

4.1	5, 4, 6, 1, 2, 3
4.2	trusted, believed, obeyed
4.3	trusted, believed, obeyed
4.4	believed, trusted, obeyed
4.5	sacrifice, lamb
4.6	Lamb, gift, sacrifice
4.7	said, promised, knew
4.8	no
4.9	yes
4.10	yes
4.11	no
4.12	to be happy
4.13	leap
4.14	to look; see
4.15	great
4.16	heaven
4.17	answers will vary
4.18	Rejoice, day, joy, behold, great, heaven

SELF TEST 4

4.01	God's rewards last forever.
4.02	God's rewards are toys.
4.03	God rewards your trust in Him.
4.04	God's rewards give joy.
4.05	God rewards everyone.
4.06	day, joy, reward, great, 6:23a
4.07	yes
4.08	yes
4.09	yes
4.010	yes
4.011	yes
4.012	right
4.013	promise
4.014	Lamb
4.015	Isaac
4.016	changes
4.017	Abraham
4.018	blessings
4.019	joy
4.020	trust Him
4.021	everything

LIFEPAC TEST

1. mountain
2. promise
3. reward
4. powerful
5. depend
6. unbelief
7. glory
8. shield
9. faith
10. provide
11. soul, waiteth
12. Lord, help
13. shield
14. son
15. joy, heaven, Jesus
16. reward, sacrifice
17. believing, trusting
18. you, everything
19. dependable
20. altar
21. sacrifice
22. Sarai
23. laughter

ALTERNATE LIFEPAC TEST

1. a place to make a sacrifice
2. a gift to God
3. a cover to protect
4. God's chosen people
5. Abraham's first name
6. Abram's wife
7. 100
8. princess
9. sorry
10. son
11. Isaac
12. nation
13. yes
14. no
15. yes
16. no
17. no
18. yes
19. son
20. altar
21. everywhere
22. sacrifice
23. faith
24. promise

BIBLE 203

ALTERNATE LIFEPAC TEST

Name _____

Date _____

My Score

19
24

Each answer = 1 point

Draw lines to match the word to the meaning.

1.	altar	▶	◀	Abram's wife
2.	sacrifice	▶	◀	God's chosen people
3.	shield	▶	◀	a place to make a sacrifice
4.	Israelites	▶	◀	a cover to protect
5.	Abram	▶	◀	a gift to God
6.	Sarai	▶	◀	Abraham's first name

Circle the correct answer.

7. When Isaac was born, Abraham was _____ years old.

50   30   100

8. Sarah's name meant _____ .

beautiful   *laughter*   *princess*

9. A sacrifice meant that people were _____ .

   happy   sad   sorry

10. God asked Abraham to sacrifice his _____ .

   cow   lamb   son

11. Abraham's son's name was _____ .

   Israel   Isaac   Moses

12. God promised Abraham a _____ .

   car   house   nation

Circle *Yes* or *No*.

13. God keeps his promises.

   Yes   No

14. A shield is a place to give a sacrifice.

   Yes   No

15. We should trust God even when we can't understand His way.

   Yes   No

16. Abraham was unwilling to sacrifice Isaac.

   Yes   No

17. Isaac carried a lamb up the mountain.

   Yes   No

18. Abraham became a great nation.

   Yes   No

Write the correct word from the box on each line.

| faith | son | sacrifice | altar | promise | everywhere |

19. God promised Abraham a _____ .

20. Abraham put Isaac on an _____ .

21. God knows everything and is always

_____ .

22. Jesus is the _____ for our sins.

23. Abraham was strong in _____ .

24. Abraham believed God's _____
of a nation.

BIBLE 204

Unit 4: How the Bible Came to Us

TEACHER NOTES

MATERIALS NEEDED FOR LIFEPAC	
Required	Suggested
• Bible	• poster board • markers or crayons • 4 × 6 index cards • Bible map • Book about the Temple

ADDITIONAL LEARNING ACTIVITIES

Section 1 - How the Old Testament Came to Us

1. Discuss these questions with your class.

   a. Do the Ten Commandments apply to us today?

   b. What are the 5 books of the Law of Moses?

   c. Who is the true author of the Bible?

   d. What are the 12 books following the Law of Moses called?

   e. Why is the next set of Bible books called "Books of Wisdom"?

   f. What is a psalm?

   g. What is a proverb?

   h. Why is the last set of Old Testament books called the "Books of the Prophets"?

   i. What do the books of the prophets tell us?

2. Teach the class the "Books of the Bible" song. Singing is a great way to memorize. In time, they will learn all of the books of the Bible in order!

3. Make a chart showing the Old Testament books by category:

   "Books of the Law," "Books of History," "Books of Wisdom," and "Books of the Prophets."

4. Study a model or print of the Temple. Locate the Holy Room mentioned by Isaiah.

5. Locate Mount Sinai on a Bible map.

6. Make a large model of the tablets from cardboard. Write the Ten Commandments on them.

Section 2 - How the New Testament Came to Us

1. Discuss these questions with your class.

   a. Who wrote the Gospels?

   b. What do the Gospels tell us?

   c. How many letters did Paul write?

   d. Who else wrote New Testament letters?

   e. What is the last book of the Bible?

2. Read excerpts (or all) of the book of Acts.
   Discuss in particular the lives of the New Testament writers.

3. Choose one or several New Testament letters to read aloud together.
   Discuss what the writer is saying, to whom it was written, and why it was written.

4. Make a game to review the New Testament. Use 4 × 6 index cards.

   On one side, write the name of the Bible book. On the other side, write a clue (or clues) about that book.

   Place all of the cards in a box. Allow the students, one at a time, to draw a card.
   He/she should read the clue(s).

   The other students try to guess the name of the Bible book.

   (Note: This game could also be played for the Old Testament books of the Bible.)

Section 3 - How the Bible Comes to Us Today

1. Display Bibles printed in languages other than English (preferably Hebrew, Greek, or Latin).

2. Read about the lives of John Wycliffe, William Tyndale, and other Bible translators.

   (Note: Historical novels can be a wonderful tool for the teacher to read aloud to the class for discussion purposes.)

   Fact and fiction must be clearly separated so the students do not become confused.

3. Visit a museum that has a display of parchment or old Bibles.

4. Have students ask their parents if they may bring in old family Bibles to compare with each other. Handle them carefully.

5. Use the Internet! Contact "theseedcompany.org" (a ministry of the Wycliffe Bible Transla-tors) to see how your class might volunteer their efforts toward spreading God's Word.

6. Invite a representative from the Gideon's to speak to your class.

Administer the LIFEPAC Test.

   The test is to be administered in one session. Give no help except with directions.
   Evaluate the tests and review areas where the students have done poorly.
   Review the pages and activities that stress the concepts tested.
   If necessary, administer the Alternate LIFEPAC Test.

ANSWER KEYS

SECTION 1

1.1	i
1.2	do
1.3	god
1.4	rest
1.5	honor
1.6	k
1.7	d
1.8	n
1.9	l
1.10	c
1.11	no
1.12	yes
1.13	no
1.14	no
1.15	yes
1.16	B
1.17	A
1.18	B
1.19	H
1.20	H
1.21	L
1.22	L
1.23	H
1.24	H
1.25	H
1.26	H
1.27	H
1.28	L
1.29	H
1.30	L
1.31	H
1.32	H
1.33	H
1.34	L
1.35	H
1.36	David
1.37	Solomon
1.38	C. Jeremiah
1.39	A. Isaiah
1.40	B. Malachi

SELF TEST 1

1.01	c
1.02	e
1.03	a
1.04	d
1.05	b
1.06	B. Moses
1.07	A. history
1.08	C. David and Solomon
1.09	C. prophets
1.010	B. Isaiah
1.011	C. Malachi
1.012	Any one: Genesis, Exodus, Leviticus, Numbers, or Deuteronomy
1.013	Any one: Joshua, Judges, Ruth, 1 or 2 Samuel, 1 or 2 Kings, 1 or 2 Chronicles, Ezra, Nehemiah, or Esther
1.014	Any one: Job, Psalms, Proverbs, Ecclesiastes, or Song of Solomon
1.015	Any one: Isaiah, Jeremiah, Lamentations, Ezekiel, Daniel, Hosea, Joel, Amos, Obadiah, Jonah, Micah, Nahum, Habakkuk, Zephaniah, Haggai, Zechariah, or Malachi

SECTION 2

2.1	A. "good news"
	Either order:
	B. Matthew
	C. John
	Any order:
	D. Luke
	E. Mark
	F. Acts
2.2	B. Jew
2.3	B. jail
2.4	C. Damascus
2.5	C. Jesus
2.6	no
2.7	yes
2.8	no
2.9	yes
2.10	yes
2.11	John
2.12	Peter
2.13	John
2.14	John

SELF TEST 2

2.01	A - apostle
2.02	C - good news
2.03	B - Paul
2.04	C - letters
2.05	B - Peter and John
2.06	yes
2.07	yes
2.08	no
2.09	yes
2.010	no
2.011	OT
2.012	NT
2.013	OT
2.014	NT
2.015	NT

SECTION 3

3.1	c
3.2	b
3.3	d
3.4	a
3.5	Promised Land
3.6	Egypt
3.7	Greek
3.8	translators
3.9	G
3.10	H
3.11	L
3.12	E
3.13	no
3.14	yes
3.15	yes
3.16	no
3.17	yes

SELF TEST 3

3.01	b
3.02	d
3.03	a
3.04	c
3.05	e
3.06	Old
3.07	New
3.08	Latin
3.09	English
3.010	Bible
3.011	<u>Bible translators are still needed today.</u>
3.012	Languages never change over time.
3.013	There is only one English translation of the Bible.
3.014	Most of the Jews in Egypt spoke English.
3.015	<u>There are still some people who do not have a Bible in their own language.</u>

LIFEPAC TEST

1. 1
2. 2
3. 1
4. 2
5. 1
6. 1
7. 2
8. 2
9. 1
10. 1
11. Ten
12. translator
13. God
14. Moses
15. Paul
16. Gospel
17. Jesus
18. John
19. English
20. Bible

ALTERNATE LIFEPAC TEST

1. C - Ten Commandments
2. C - five books
3. A - Psalms
4. B - Jeremiah
5. A - Malachi
6. B
7. D
8. A
9. E
10. C
11. Gospel
12.-13. Either order:
    Matthew
    John
14.-16. Any order:
    Mark
    Luke
    Acts
17. G
18. H
19. L
20. E

BIBLE 204

ALTERNATE LIFEPAC TEST

Name _____

Date _____

My Score

16

20

Each answer = 1 point

Circle the correct answer.

1. God gave Moses the _____ .
    a. Ten Good Ideas
    b. Ten Suggestions
    c. Ten Commandments

2. The Law of Moses contains _____ book(s).
    a. one
    b. three
    c. five

3. King David wrote many of the songs in the Book of _____ .
    a. Psalms
    b. Proverbs
    c. Job

4.   The prophet _____ wrote the books of Jeremiah and Lamentations.
     a.   Lamentation
     b.   Jeremiah
     c.   Amos

5.   The Book of _____ is the last book of the Old Testament.
     a.   Malachi
     b.   Hosea
     c.   Joel

Draw lines to match the words and definitions.

6.   apostle ▶

7.   author ▶

8.   prophet ▶

9.   throne ▶

10. translator ▶

a.   one who speaks for God

b.   follower of Jesus chosen by Him to preach the Gospel

c.   one who changes speech or writing from one language to another

d.   one who originally thinks of a story and the words to use

e.   special chair for a king

Read each word in the box.

Then write each word under the best heading.

Gospel	Mark	Matthew	Luke	Acts	John

Good News	Books written by the Apostles	Books written by friends of Apostles
11. _____	12. _____	14. _____
	13. _____	15. _____
		16. _____

Write H for Hebrew, L for Latin, E for English, G for Greek.

17. _____ At the time of Jesus and the early church, most *Christians* read the Old Testament in this language.

18. _____ The *Jews* continued to make copies of the Old Testament in this language.

19. _____ About 200 years after Christ, many people in the Roman Empire spoke this language.

20. _____ In this language, one of the most famous Bible translations is the King James Version.

BIBLE 205

Unit 5: *Z-Z-Z-Zing!* Went David's Sling

TEACHER NOTES

MATERIALS NEEDED FOR LIFEPAC	
Required	Suggested
(None)	• Bible • teaching pictures of the life of Daniel

ADDITIONAL LEARNING ACTIVITIES

Section 1 - David and the Sheep

1. Discuss these questions with your class.

   a. Why do sheep need to be watched more closely than other animals?

   b. Would it really be possible to kill a bear or lion by hand? (Note: Students may wish to research the relative strength of these animals in a reference book or online.)

2. Research the occupation of sheepherding. Was a shepherd in Bible times very different from a shepherd today?

3. Read about the Basque shepherds of Spain.

4. Locate Bethlehem on a Bible map.

5. Read about sheep in a reference book or online.

6. Make a sling from leather thongs and a scrap of heavy cloth.

Section 2 - David and Two Great Men

1. Discuss why David was chosen to be king rather than one of his older brothers.

2. Plan a dramatization showing David's brothers appearing before Samuel, the confusion of Jesse, and finally the sending for David.

3. Write or tell of a time when you were misled by looking at the outward appearance of a person or item.

Section 3 - David and the Giant

1. Discuss these questions with your class.

   a. Was Goliath a bully? Why?

   b. Should God's people have been afraid of Goliath?

   c. Were David's brothers right in thinking him a show-off?

2. Divide the students into two groups. Let the first group tell of the things Goliath had to make him strong. Let the second group tell of David.

3. Discuss whether David or Goliath was really stronger and give reasons why.

4. Discuss whether we can be as strong as David or Goliath and in what ways.

5. How tall was Goliath? Can you find out how much his armor and other equipment weighed?

ANSWER KEYS

SECTION 1

1.1 sheep
1.2 father
1.3 Bethlehem
1.4 God
1.5 shepherd
1.6 Teacher check, no
1.7 God
1.8 risked
1.9 (any order)
       We can't get near the sheep! David watches all the time!
       Don't go near David and his sheep!
       He doesn't miss with his sling!
       Oo-Ooo-- did that rock hurt!
       He killed a bear.
       He saved a lamb from the lion, then killed the lion!
       It's hard to believe, but David will risk his life for even one sheep!
       I just about had that fat black lamb, and -Whoosh! I was hit by David's staff... Ohh poor me.
       Did you hear David play his harp today?
       He was singing, too.
1.10 lamb, lion, God, bear
1.11 Teacher check
1.12 Teacher check
1.13 sheep believe meat cheer creep beat sleep baby deer hungry field funny
1.14 a. creep, steep
       b. bake, lake
       c. seat, street
       d. told, hold
       e. ride, slide
       f. stole, hole
       g. fight, bite

SELF TEST 1

1.01 yes
1.02 yes
1.03 child
1.04 He was a shepherd
1.05 He loved God.
1.06 He was lazy.
1.07 He played the harp
1.08 He risked his life for his sheep.
1.09 He fought bears and lions.
1.010 Jesse
1.011 Bethlehem
1.012 about God

SECTION 2

2.1	Drawings will vary.
2.2	prophet
2.3	God
2.4	anoint, dinner, lion, Samuel, Prophet, oil, ten
2.5	Teacher check
2.6	Samuel Anoints David
2.7	heart and mind
2.8	a. he was gentle
	b. he sang about God's love
	c. he obeyed his father
	e. he worked hard
2.9	Bethlehem
2.10	Israel
2.11	150
2.12	Teacher check
2.13	doings
2.14	middle
2.15	Proverbs 20:11
2.16	the sheep
2.17	Jesse
2.18	God
2.19	Saul's helper
2.20	Saul
2.21	lions and bears
2.22	day, age, eight, sleigh, stray, way, late, tail, make, chain, pain

2.23

Long A:	Long E:
a. gate	a. eagle
b. stay	b. steep
c. mail	c. field
d. train	d. seat
e. weigh	e. lonely

SELF TEST 2

2.01	prophet
2.02	yes
2.03	heart and mind
2.04	doings
2.05	Saul
2.06	prophet
2.07	David
2.08	Psalm
2.09	Bethlehem
2.010	The Psalms are near the middle of the Bible.
2.011	King Saul had bad dreams.
2.012	God's blessing was on David.
2.013	Samuel anointed Jesse.
2.014	David risked his life for his sheep.
2.015	David sang songs about God.
2.016	God
2.017	Proverbs

SECTION 3

3.1 Saul
3.2 Goliath
3.3 God
3.4 Philistines
3.5 ten
3.6 Drawings will vary.
3.7 yes
3.8 G
3.9 G
3.10 D
3.11 G
3.12 G
3.13 D
3.14 D
3.15 Jesse
3.16 Samuel
3.17 Saul
3.18 ng
3.19 ld
3.20 nt
3.21 nk
3.22 mp
3.23 st
3.24 mb
3.25 sk
3.26 Teacher check
3.27 Even a child is known by his doings.
3.28 Drawings will vary.

SELF TEST 3

3.01 shepherd
3.02 Bethlehem
3.03 prophet
3.04 David
3.05 sling
3.06 God
3.07 a harp
3.08 David's songs made Saul feel better
3.09 child, doings
3.010 David had practiced with his sling.
3.011 Goliath was afraid.
3.012 God was David's helper.
3.013 Goliath was too big.
3.014 enemies of Israel
3.015 King of Israel
3.016 a Philistine giant
3.017 a prophet of God
3.018 David's father
3.019 country where David lived
3.020 yes
3.021 yes
3.022
3.023 yes
3.024 yes

LIFEPAC TEST

1. Jesse
2. Samuel
3. Saul
4. Goliath
5. Bethlehem
6. David
7. yes
8. yes
9. yes
10. no
11. yes
12. no
13. anoint David
14. a king
15. heart and mind
16. prophet
17. God
18. b. David had practiced with his sling.
    d. God was David's helper
19. child, doings
20. God

ALTERNATE LIFEPAC TEST

1. musical instrument
2. metal hat
3. stone thrower
4. long-handled knife
5. shepherd's stick
6. Jesse
7. seven
8. prophet
9. giant
10. middle
11. yes
12. no
13. no
14. no
15. yes
16. Goliath
17. David
18. Jesse
19. Samuel
20. God

BIBLE 205

ALTERNATE LIFEPAC TEST

Name _____

Date _____

My Score

16
20

Each answer = 1 point

Draw lines to match.

1.	harp ▶		◀ shepherd's stick
2.	helmet ▶		◀ stone thrower
3.	sling ▶		◀ long-handled knife
4.	spear ▶		◀ musical instrument
5.	staff ▶		◀ metal hat

Circle the correct answer.

6. David's father was _____ .

   Goliath   Jesse   Solomon

7. David had _____ brothers.

   two   ten   seven

8. Someone who spoke for God was a _____ .

   prophet   helper   king

9. Goliath was a _____ .

   bear   giant   king

10. Psalms is near the _____ of the Bible.

    middle   beginning   end

Answer *yes* or *no*.

11. _____ Goliath was a Philistine.
12. _____ David lived in Nazareth.
13. _____ David was anointed to be a prophet.
14. _____ The Philistines were short people.
15. _____ When David played his harp, the king felt better.

Write the correct name from the box on each line.

Samuel	God	David	Jesse	Goliath

16. _____ made fun of God.
17. _____ came in the name of the Lord.
18. _____ had eight sons.
19. _____ knew a secret.
20. _____ looks at the heart.

BIBLE 206

Unit 6: God Is Everywhere

TEACHER NOTES

MATERIALS NEEDED FOR LIFEPAC	
Required	Suggested
(None)	• Bible

ADDITIONAL LEARNING ACTIVITIES

Section 1 - Understanding God

1. Discuss the stars. Do we see the same stars today as the first stars made? Do stars move?
2. Plan a trip to an observatory or invite a guest with a telescope to talk to the class about stars.
3. Make a chart locating some of the major stars.
4. Research how stars are used for navigation.
5. Research the effect of the moon and the stars on the tides.

Section 2 - Understanding Creation

1. Find examples, other than the examples in your LIFEPAC, of fish or animals in God's system.
2. Make six 8" circles from construction paper. Use one circle to represent each day of creation. On each circle, name and illustrate God's creations for that day. Ask your parents or older brother or sister to help you.

Section 3 - Understanding God's Will

1. Discuss whether or not it is possible to hide or run away from God.
2. Pantomime Jonah's trip on the boat.
3. Locate Nineveh and Tarshish on a Bible map. Where did Jonah travel?
4. Research fish. Would it be possible to live inside one?

Administer the LIFEPAC Test.

> The test is to be administered in one session. Give no help except with directions.
> Evaluate the tests and review areas where the students have done poorly.
> Review the pages and activities that stress the concepts tested.
> If necessary, administer the Alternate LIFEPAC Test.

ANSWER KEYS

SECTION 1

1.1	Answers will vary.
1.2	Answers will vary.
1.3	January 1
1.4	March 21
1.5	Teacher check
1.6	no
1.7	no
1.8	no
1.9	yes
1.10	yes
1.11	no
1.12	yes
1.13	yes
1.14	no
1.15	yes
1.16	no
1.17	yes
1.18	yes
1.19	yes
1.20	yes
1.21	Jesus Christ
1.22	yes
1.23	to make known
1.24	the heavens
1.25	the sky
1.26	work done by hand
1.27	heavens, glory, God, firmament, handiwork; Teacher check
1.28	**words with circle:** rain, tails
1.29	**words with box:** sea, heat, beat, leaves, eat, really, treat

1.30

seat:	head:	steak:
please	heavy	steak
leaves	head	great
seat	ready	break
each	bread	
sea		
east		
clean		
leap		

1.31	before
1.32	no
1.33	no
1.34	to eat mother's cookies
1.35	yes
1.36	yes
1.37	Dad
1.38	To make something that has not been made before.

SELF TEST 1

1.01	before the beginning.
1.02	things that work together.
1.03	from what God created.
1.04	the glory of God.
1.05	is to create.
1.06	heavens, glory, God, handiwork
1.07	handiwork
1.08	create
1.09	sky
1.010	stars and moon
1.011	light
1.012	God
1.013	no
1.014	yes
1.015	yes
1.016	yes
1.017	no
1.018	yes

SECTION 2

2.1   face, body
2.2   clearly
2.3   made
2.4 & 2.5

(took)   toot
(cook)   fool
spoon   loop
balloon   (look)
(foot)   (wood)
[poor]   [floor]

2.6, 2.7, & 2.8

moon:	book:	door:
spoon	took	poor
balloon	cook	floor
toot	foot	
fool	look	
loop	wood	

2.9   every, season, time, purpose, heaven, 1
2.10   Answers will vary.
2.11   Teacher check
2.12   family
2.13   They watch the baby lions play.
2.14   They make them go out among the fierce animals.
2.15   They teach them to fly.
2.16   The parents spank the little bears when they are bad.
2.17   yes
2.18   thing, season, purpose, heaven, Ecclesiastes
2.19   flying away quickly, eating bugs
2.20   Answers will vary.
2.21   Answers will vary.
2.22   Teacher check
2.23   To every thing there is a season, and a time to every purpose under heaven.
2.24   yes
2.25   yes
2.26   yes
2.27   yes
2.28   yes
2.29   Teacher check
2.30   Teacher check
2.31   Teacher check

SELF TEST 2

2.01   yes
2.02   yes
2.03   yes
2.04   no
2.05   no
2.06   yes
2.07   yes
2.08   yes
2.09   oxpecker
2.010   fly
2.011   God
2.012   season
2.013   heaven
2.014   God
2.015   handiwork
2.016   helper plan
2.017   family plan
2.018   invisible
2.019   plant and animal plan
2.020   family plan

SECTION 3

3.1	yes
3.2	no
3.3	yes
3.4	no
3.5	yes
3.6	read
3.7	farm
3.8	run
3.9	clean
3.10	warm
3.11	The people on the ship threw Jonah into the sea.
3.12	A big fish swallowed Jonah.
3.13	Jonah was in the big fish three days and three nights.
3.14	God made the fish spit Jonah out.
3.15	Jonah went to Nineveh.
3.16	Punish them in forty days.
3.17	They stopped sinning.
3.18	Answers will vary.
3.19	Answers will vary.
3.20	faster
3.21	prettiest
3.22	funniest
3.23	bigger
3.24	longest

3.25

scr:	sl:
scream	slope
scrape	slick
scrub	sleep
screen	slip
scratch	slam

3.26	5
3.27	1
3.28	4
3.29	2
3.30	3
3.31	6

SELF TEST 3

3.01	want
3.02	God
3.03	Jonah
3.04	stormy
3.05	God
3.06	before
3.07	watch
3.08	no
3.09	yes
3.010	yes
3.011	no
3.012	yes
3.013	no
3.014	yes
3.015	every, season, time, purpose, heaven
3.016	heavens, glory, God, firmament, handiwork
3.017	excuse
3.018	family
3.019	rhinoceros
3.020	Son

LIFEPAC TEST

1. make something that has not been made before.
2. what God created.
3. before the beginning.
4. work together.
5. to do God's will.
6. to go to Nineveh.
7. God
8. rhinoceros
9. Son
10. plants
11. car
12. Nineveh
13. heavens, glory, God, firmament, handiwork
14. season, time, purpose, heaven
15. yes
16. yes
17. yes
18. no
19. yes
20. no
21.

God created	**People make**
plants	cars
world	houses
families	chairs
sky	
trees	
animals	

ALTERNATE LIFEPAC TEST

1. systems
2. create
3. roots
4. heaven
5. moon
6. families
7. days
8. no
9. yes
10. no
11. no
12. no
13. yes
14. yes
15. yes
16. heavens, handiwork
17. beginning, heaven, earth

BIBLE 206

ALTERNATE LIFEPAC TEST

Name _____

Date _____

My Score

14 / 17

Each answer = 1 point

Write the correct word from the box on each line.

roots	systems	families	heaven	days	moon	create

1. Things that work together are called _____ .

2. To make something never made before is to

    _____ .

3. The part of the plant that is underground is called the

    _____ .

4. *Firmament* is another word for _____ .

5. Water is made to move by the pull of the _____ .

6. Both animals and people have the system of

    _____ .

7. Jonah was in the fish three _____

Answer yes or no.

8. _____ All snowflakes have the same shape.

9. _____ Mudskippers can climb trees.

10. _____ The oxpecker is a kind of rhinoceros.

11. _____ Nineveh was the name of a ship.

12. _____ God was born before He created the world.

13. _____ God loved the world so much He gave His Son for the world.

14. _____ When Jonah was thrown into the sea, the storm stopped.

15. _____ God made the fish spit Jonah out on dry land.

Write the correct word from the Memory verses on each line.

16. "The _____ declare the glory

of God; and the firmament showeth His

_____ ."

Psalm 19:1

17. "In the _____ God created the

_____ and the _____ ."

Genesis 1:1

BIBLE 207

Unit 7: The Story of Joseph

TEACHER NOTES

MATERIALS NEEDED FOR LIFEPAC	
Required	Suggested
• Bible	• Bible map • construction paper • cloth strips • flat stones • grain • heavy cream • jar with lid

ADDITIONAL LEARNING ACTIVITIES

Section 1 - Joseph as a Boy

1. Discuss these questions with your class.

   a. How do you feel about parents "playing favorites" with one child in the family?

   b. Is it possible for parents to treat all the children, no matter what their ages, exactly the same? Why or why not?

   c. If a child shows more responsibility and loyalty than his brothers and sisters, should he be given special privileges? Why or why not?

   d. Would you like your parents to tell all the children in your family why they are treated as they are?

   e. Where did people live in Joseph's time?

   f. What kinds of food did they eat?

   g. Where did they get it?

   h. How did people get their clothes?

   i. How did people worship God in Joseph's time?

   j. How was sin dealt with in Joseph's day?

   k. How is sin dealt with today?

   l. Was life easier or harder in Joseph's day? Explain your answer.

2. Make a picture or model of Joseph's coat with various colors of construction paper or cloth strips.

3. Visit a historic park or museum to see how life was lived in ancient times.

4. Visit a natural history museum to learn more about archaeology.

5. Have "Joseph Day"!

   Allow the students to dress in Bible clothing.
   Grind grain.
   Make butter.
   Sit around an imaginary campfire and share Old Testament stories and their lessons.
   Write on a clay tablet.

6. On "Joseph Day" allow children to portray various craftsmen. Let the other children guess who is being portrayed.

Section 2 - Joseph as a Man

1. Discuss these questions with your class.

   a. Why were Joseph's brothers jealous of him?

   b. Was anyone ever jealous of you?
      How did he/she treat you?
      What did you do?
      What would God want you to do?

   c. What do you think would have happened to Joseph's family if he had not been sold as a slave and had not gone to Egypt?

   d. Why was Joseph given a position of responsibility in Egypt, especially since he was a foreigner?

   e. How do you think Joseph was able to love and forgive his brothers after what they did to him?

2. Act out the dinner Joseph prepared for his brothers and the scene in which Joseph revealed himself to his brothers.

3. On a Bible map, find Joseph's home and trace his trip to Egypt.

4. Find the land of Goshen on a Bible map.

5. Encourage the students to write or tell about a time when they were able to forgive someone who hurt them.

6. Watch and discuss an age-appropriate video about the life of Joseph.

7. Practice vocabulary and definitions before each test.
   Divide the class into teams.
   Write a vocabulary word on the board.
   Who can give the correct definition first?

Administer the LIFEPAC Test.

   The test is to be administered in one session. Give no help except with directions.
   Evaluate the tests and review areas where the students have done poorly.
   Review the pages and activities that stress the concepts tested.
   If necessary, administer the Alternate LIFEPAC Test.

ANSWER KEYS

SECTION 1

1.1	b.	Jacob and Rachel
1.2	c.	ten
1.3	b.	one
1.4	a.	Genesis
1.5	c.	Archaeologists
1.6		Teacher check
1.7		mats
1.8		hooks
1.9		Curtains
1.10		meal / times
1.11		out / side
1.12		every / one
1.13		some / times
1.14	c.	small clay pot that held oil
1.15	d.	told stories about God and his ancestors.
1.16	b.	have faith and trust God
1.17	a.	covered up with his coat.
1.18		farmer
1.19		shepherd
1.20		carpenter
1.21		mason
1.22		potter
1.23		tanner
1.24		clay tablet
1.25		stylus
1.26		Teacher check
1.27		Family check
1.28		orship
1.29		ones
1.30		ather
1.31		ather
1.32		others
1.33		acrificed
1.34		ins
1.35		Teacher check

SELF TEST 1

1.01	yes
1.02	no
1.03	no
1.04	no
1.05	yes
1.06	oil
1.07	Ancestors
1.08	mats
1.09	oxen
1.010	altar
1.011	loved
	gave
	Son
	Him
	life

SECTION 2

2.1 Teacher check
2.2 4
2
5
1
3
2.3 a. traders
2.4 c. Judah
2.5 b. slave
2.6 c. God
2.7 yes
2.8 no
2.9 yes
2.10 no
2.11 trade
2.12 work
2.13 like
2.14 bless
2.15 listen
2.16 pray
2.17 plan
2.18 b. dream
2.19 b. meat
2.20 c. mean
2.21 c. beans
2.22 seven
2.23 seven
2.24 famine
2.25 ruler
2.26 food
2.27 God
2.28 save
2.29 b. upset or worried
2.30 f. angry at something unfair
2.31 c. more than enough
2.32 a. one who buys and sells
2.33 d. king of Egypt
2.34 h. one in charge of a place and its people
2.35 g. to know much about something
2.36 e. stalk of cut grain bound together
2.37 Teacher check
2.38 Teacher check

SELF TEST 2

2.01 e. A special place to worship God
2.02 c. One who buys and sells
2.03 d. To make an offering of something valuable
2.04 a. One who studied past human life
2.05 b. Extreme lack of food
2.06 wise
2.07 jealous
2.08 sad
2.09 disturbed
2.010 sorry
2.011 afraid
trust
2.012 all
good
love
2.013 brothers
2.014 Jacob
2.015 Pharaoh's servant
2.016 Pharaoh
2.017 Joseph

LIFEPAC TEST

1. had a dream
2. went to prison
3. did not go to a school
4. had a pretty coat
5. ate at a table
6. jumped in a well
7. rode on a camel
8. prayed to God
9. would sleep on a bed
10. put food away for the people
11. box
12. jar
13. apple
14. prison
15. yes
16. yes
17. yes
18. yes
19. no
20. Genesis
21. famine
22. sins
23. stones
24. oil
25. good

ALTERNATE LIFEPAC TEST

1. yes
2. no
3. no
4. no
5. yes
6. b. at a rock altar
7. c. father
8. a. Jacob
9. b. an old well
10. c. Egypt
11. afraid
    trust
12. all
    good
    love
13. c. special place to worship God
14. f. family relative who lived long ago
15. i. job which needs special skill with one's hands
16. a. extreme lack of food
17. j. to be angry at something unfair
18. g. king in ancient Egypt
19. b. more than enough
20. e. an offering of something valuable
21. h. to know much about something
22. d. to pray to God and praise Him

BIBLE 207

ALTERNATE LIFEPAC TEST

Name _____

Date _____

My Score

20 / 25

Each answer = 1 point

Answer *yes* or *no*.

1. _____ Joseph's father and mother were Jacob and Rachel.

2. _____ Joseph's story is found in the book of Leviticus in the Bible.

3. _____ Biologists study the lives of people who lived long ago.

4. _____ A potter made and fixed farm tools.

5. _____ A trader is one who buys and sells.

Circle the correct answer.

6. Joseph and his family worshipped God _____ .

   a. in a church

   b. at a rock alter

   c. by the water

7. Joseph's _____ taught him about God and work.

    a. mother

    b. brother

    c. father

8. _____ gave Joseph a coat of many colors.

    a. Jacob

    b. Rachel

    c. Reuben

9. Joseph's brothers threw him into _____ .

    a. a stream

    b. an old well

    c. a pit

10. Joseph became ruler of all of _____ .

    a. America

    b. Europe

    c. Egypt

Write the missing words in the blanks to finish the Bible verses.

11. "What time I am _____ , I will

_____ in thee [God]."

Psalm 56:3

12. "And we know that _____ things work

together for _____ to them that

_____ God, to them who are the called

according to his purpose."

Romans 8:28

Draw a line to match each word with its meaning.

13.	altar ▸	**a.** extreme lack of food
14.	ancestor ▸	**b.** more than enough
15.	a trade ▸	**c.** special place to worship God
16.	famine ▸	**d.** to pray to God and praise Him
17.	jealous ▸	**e.** an offering of something valuable
18.	Pharaoh ▸	**f.** family relative who lived long ago
19.	plenty ▸	**g.** king in ancient Egypt
20.	sacrifice ▸	**h.** to know much about something
21.	wise ▸	**i.** job which needs special skill with one's hands
22.	worship ▸	**j.** to be angry at something unfair

BIBLE 208

Unit 8: God and the Family

TEACHER NOTES

MATERIALS NEEDED FOR LIFEPAC	
Required	Suggested
(None)	• Bible • crayons or colored pencils

ADDITIONAL LEARNING ACTIVITIES

Section 1 - God Made the Family

1. Discuss these questions with your class.

    a. Why does God want men and women to get married?

    b. Did Isaac pick Rebekah to be his wife? Why not?

    c. Why did Isaac love Rebekah?

2. Ask someone to read Genesis, Chapter 24, to you if you cannot read it all for yourself. Make a little play in three scenes.

    Scene 1. Abraham sends his servant to find a bride for Isaac.

    Scene 2. The servant at Nahor's house.

    Scene 3. Isaac meets his bride.

3. On a big sheet of paper, draw your "family tree" back as far as you can. You will need to ask your father or mother to help you.

    A suggested start: <u>your name</u>

    <u>your father's name</u>   <u>your mother's name</u>

    <u>father's father</u>   <u>father's mother</u>   <u>mother's father</u>   <u>mother's mother</u>

Section 2 - God Wants Happy Families

1. Discuss these questions with your class.

    a. What is it that makes a family happy as the members live and work together?

    b. What does the Bible say is the father's most important job—more important even than earning the living?

2. Have a student go to the chalkboard and write a list of "family" words as the other students take turns calling them out (examples: *love, help*).

3. With the help of an adult, use a Bible concordance (printed or online) to find all of the commandments given specifically to children.
    Note: Look under *children* in an unabridged concordance such as *Strong's*.

Section 3 - God Loves Children

1. Discuss these questions with your class.

    a. What commandment did God give that was specifically for children?

    b. What does the Bible mean when it says, "Honor thy father and mother"?

    c. What is the first duty of children in the family?

    d. Besides obeying, what other things can children do to honor their parents?

2. As a group, make a list of things parents ask you to do that you find hardest to obey. Share with each other ways in which you have improved your readiness to obey.

Administer the LIFEPAC Test.

The test is to be administered in one session. Give no help except with directions.
Evaluate the tests and review areas where the students have done poorly.
Review the pages and activities that stress the concepts tested.
If necessary, administer the Alternate LIFEPAC Test.

ANSWER KEYS

SECTION 1

1.1	world
1.2	friend
1.3	Adam
1.4	named
1.5	alone
1.6	woman
1.7	Eve
1.8	wife
1.9	rib
1.10	family
1.11	husband
1.12	wife
1.13	family
1.14	Teacher check
1.15	married
1.16	wife
1.17	woman
1.18	each other
1.19	Adam, Eve
1.20	three
1.21	Cain, Abel, and Seth
1.22	Cain
1.23	so there will always be people on the earth
1.24	Teacher check
1.25	yes
1.26	yes
1.27	yes
1.28	no
1.29	Abraham believed God. The baby's name was Isaac. God kept His promise.
1.30	Isaac
1.31	Rebekah
1.32	servant

1.33	gold
1.34	old
1.35	Teacher check
1.36	Isaac
1.37	sadder, saddest
1.38	hotter, hottest
1.39	madder, maddest
1.40	wetter, wettest
1.41	bigger, biggest
1.42	biggest
1.43	hottest
1.44	fatter
1.45	madder
1.46	sadder
1.47	Teacher check
1.48	Abraham
1.49	Abraham
1.50	yes
1.51	yes
1.52	Jacob and Esau
1.53	Jacob and Esau
1.54	grandfather
1.55	father
1.56	grandchild
1.57	twins
1.58	mother
1.59	father
1.60	great-grandfather
1.61	grandfather
1.62	father
1.63	grandchildren

SELF TEST 1

1.01 God
1.02 Adam
1.03 Eve
1.04 a rib or Adam's rib
1.05 Cain, Abel, and Seth
1.06 husband
1.07 wife
1.08 twins
1.09 grandfather
1.010 friend
1.011 helper
1.012 wife

1.013 husband
1.014 married
1.015 family
1.016 yes
1.017 yes
1.018 yes
1.019 no
1.020 yes
1.021 yes
1.022 no
1.023 no
1.024 yes
1.025 no
1.026 yes

SECTION 2

2.1	love, help
2.2	love, help
2.3	(any order)
	take children to church
	go to work
	read the Bible
	be the leader of the family
	love mother
	teach children about God
2.4	a. knocks
	b. knife
	c. knit
	d. wrap
	e. wring
	f. wreck
2.5	a. k
	b. k
	c. k
	d. w
	e. w
	f. w
2.6	Teacher check
2.7	Teacher check
2.8	make your bed
	sweep the floor
	watch the baby
	carry out the trash
	pick up toys
	hang up your shirts
	help put away dishes
	set the table
	dust
	feed the dog
2.9	Teacher check
2.10	obey, love, help, help
2.11	Teacher check
2.12	Miriam watched the basket.
2.13	Teacher check
2.14	king
2.15	boy
2.16	mother
2.17	basket
2.18	sister
2.19	Miriam
2.20	daughter
2.21	Teacher check
2.22	needs
2.23	feed
2.24	meat
2.25	weed
2.26	sleeps
2.27	three
2.28	steal

SELF TEST 2

2.01	happy
2.02	love, help
2.03	child, known, doings
2.04	mothers
2.05	children
2.06	fathers
2.07	fathers
2.08	children
2.09	mothers
2.010	fathers
2.011	mothers, fathers, or children
2.012	mothers or fathers
2.013	married
2.014	each other
2.015	grandfather
2.016	brothers
2.017	fathers and mothers

SECTION 3

3.1	obey
3.2	Teacher check
3.3	true
3.4	not true
3.5	true
3.6	not true
3.7	true
3.8	not true
3.9	true
3.10	true
3.11	not true
3.12	Teacher check
3.13	life, good, long, obey, man
3.14	good long life, obey
3.15	Honour thy father and mother; which is the first commandment with promise; That is may be well with thee, and thou mayest live long on the earth. Ephesians 6:2 and 3.
3.16	Teacher check
3.17	Teacher check
3.18	Teacher check
3.19	Teacher check
3.20	did not obey
3.21	did not obey
3.22	Teacher check
3.23	Teacher check
3.24	Teacher check
3.25	no
3.26	no
3.27	yes
3.28	no
3.29	no
3.30	Billy had to go to the doctor with his mother.
3.31	He couldn't play with Billy for a whole week.
3.32	no
3.33	yes
3.34	Example: So he will be safe. So she will know where he is.
3.35	yes
3.36	yes
3.37	yes
3.38	no
3.39	yes
3.40	yes
3.41	2
3.42	3
3.43	1
3.44	4
3.45	5
3.46	Teacher check

SELF TEST 3

3.01	mother and father
3.02	obey
3.03	a law
3.04	a person's word
3.05	matters a lot
3.06	feel good inside
3.07	Honor thy father and mother; which is the first commandment with promise; That it may be well with thee, and thou mayest live long on the earth.
3.08	true
3.09	true
3.010	true
3.011	true
3.012	not true
3.013	not true
3.014	true
3.015	love, help
3.016	married
3.017	brothers
3.018	fathers
3.019	mothers
3.020	children
3.021	Eve
3.022	servant
3.023	married
3.024	church

LIFEPAC TEST

1. mother and father
2. Abraham's son
3. the first baby
4. the first man
5. obey
6. Abraham's grandchildren
7. Isaac's wife
8. made from a rib
9. true
10. true
11. not true
12. not true
13. true
14. true
15. not true
16. woman
17. love
18. obey
19. well
20. grandfather
21. doings
22. Honor thy father and mother; which is the first commandment with promise; That it may be well with thee, and thou mayest live long on the earth.

ALTERNATE LIFEPAC TEST

1. parents
2. Cain
3. wife
4. Isaac
5. twins
6. father
7. not true
8. not true
9. true
10. true
11. not true
12. true
13. Miriam, brother
14. servant
15. family
16. Either order: love, help
17. Eve
18. obeying
19. gets married
20. grandfather
21. the church
22. Adam

BIBLE 208
ALTERNATE LIFEPAC TEST

Name _____

Date _____

My Score

19
24

Each answer = 1 point

Draw lines to match the words.

1. mother and father ▸   ◂ twins

2. first baby ▸   ◂ Isaac

3. the woman a man
    marries ▸   ◂ father

4. Rebekah's husband ▸   ◂ parents

5. Abraham's
    grandchildren ▸   ◂ Cain

6. leader of the family ▸   ◂ wife

Answer *true* or *not true*.

7. _____ Children should not help the family until they are big.

8. _____ Fathers should love mothers like a car.

9. _____ Mothers should help fathers.

10. _____ Abraham's family grew to become many families.

11. _____ Sarah was the first woman.

12. _____ Obeying your parents is sometimes hard.

Write the best word on each line. Use words from the box.

obeying	brother	family	help
Miriam	love	Eve	servant

13. _____ was a big sister who watched her little _____ .

14. Isaac's wife was brought to him by a _____ .

15. A father, mother, and children make a _____ .

16. God made families to _____ and _____ one another.

17. The mother of Seth was _____ .

18. A child can show his love for God by _____ his parents.

Draw a circle around the best word to finish the sentence.

19.   A new family begins when someone _____ .

has a birthday   gets married   gets a job

20.   Your father's father is your _____ .

brother   uncle   grandfather

21.   Fathers should love mothers like God loves _____ .

little children   the church   the world

22.   The first father was _____ .

Jacob   Adam   Abraham

BIBLE 209

Unit 9: God Made the Nations

TEACHER NOTES

MATERIALS NEEDED FOR LIFEPAC	
Required	Suggested
(None)	• Bible

ADDITIONAL LEARNING ACTIVITIES

Section 1 - Babel's Great Tower

1. Discuss how high a building would have to be to reach heaven. Would such a building 0be possible to construct?

2. Why was God sad that the people were trying to build a tower to heaven?

3. With scraps of styrofoam or sugar cubes, construct your version of the Tower of Babel.

Section 2 - God's Great Nation

1. Try to arrange for someone who speaks another language to come to address your class.

2. Discuss why groups that did not speak the same language moved apart.

3. Try to bring to class recordings of speaking or singing in a different language. Can you understand any of the words?

4. See if you are able to find the approximate numbers of nations and languages in the world today. With the help of an adult, look in an encyclopedia, the World Almanac, or CIA *The World Factbook* online.

Section 3 - Our Great Task

1. Discuss this question with your class: Why is it harder to tell the Good News to people now than it would have been before the Tower of Babel?

2. On a piece of poster board, or something similar, letter the words, GO GIVE PRAY, to remind you what you can do now to do God's great task.

Administer the LIFEPAC Test.

The test is to be administered in one session. Give no help except with directions.
Evaluate the tests and review areas where the students have done poorly.
Review the pages and activities that stress the concepts tested.
If necessary, administer the Alternate LIFEPAC Test.

ANSWER KEYS

SECTION 1

1.1	yes
1.2	yes
1.3	power
1.4	tower
1.5	seven
1.6	heaven
1.7	the people were proud
1.8	everyone's words were mixed up
1.9	mixed up
1.10	to show their power.
1.11	God
1.12	Babel
1.13	power
1.14	heaven
1.15	language
1.16	languages
1.17	understand
1.18	mixed up
1.19	stop
1.20	fall
1.21	God
1.22	store
1.23	farm
1.24	dark
1.25	corn
1.26	bark

SELF TEST 1

1.01	tower
1.02	heaven
1.03	mixed up
1.04	proud
1.05	languages
1.06	power
1.07	proud
1.08	power
1.09	great
1.010	together
1.011	languages
1.012	fall
1.013	Babel
1.014	yes
1.015	no
1.016	no
1.017	no
1.018	yes
1.019	yes
1.020	yes

SECTION 2

2.1	2
2.2	1
2.3	4
2.4	3
2.5	zip
2.6	quack
2.7	fox
2.8	visit
2.9	five
2.10	fix
2.11	quiet
2.12	zoom
2.13	God gave Abraham a promise.
2.14	God wanted to hurt Abraham's family.
2.15	Abraham's family became the United States.
2.16	Jesus was going to be born into Abraham's family.
2.17	Abraham was to have a large family.
2.18	Jews
2.19	Israel
2.20	Hebrew
2.21	Teacher check
2.22	Jesus
2.23	God
2.24	Jews
2.25	Hebrew
2.26	God promised his family would become a great nation. Jesus would be born into his family.
2.27	I will
2.28	I am
2.29	I have
2.30	they are
2.31	they will
2.32	we have
2.33	I am
2.34	we are
2.35	you are
2.36	you will
2.37	we will
2.38	they have

SELF TEST 2

2.01	no
2.02	yes
2.03	yes
2.04	yes
2.05	yes
2.06	yes
2.07	no
2.08	power
2.09	languages
2.010	nations
2.011	Israel
2.012	Jews
2.013	Hebrew
2.014	Jesus
2.015	were very proud
2.016	reach heaven
2.017	the tower
2.018	would be a great nation
2.019	Jews
2.020	God

SECTION 3

3.1 Teacher check
3.2 Teacher check
3.3 Jesus
3.4 Israel
3.5 baby
3.6 nations
3.7 The answer depends on the child.
Any answer or no answer is correct.
3.8 Jesus
3.9 Hebrew
3.10 God's Word
3.11 tower
3.12 About five languages are in the world today. **X**
3.13 In some nations people pray to gods made of stone.
3.14 Jesus was a Jew.
3.15 Chinese writing looks just like ours. **X**
3.16 teach, alway, world, 28
3.17 Teacher check
3.18 Teacher check
3.19 people
3.20 Jesus
3.21 Israel
3.22 nations
3.23 Jesus told us to tell others about Him.
3.24 est
3.25 ly
3.26 er
3.27 ly
3.28 est
3.29 er

SELF TEST 3

3.01 fall
3.02 languages
3.03 Jews
3.04 people
3.05 Jesus
3.06 stone
3.07 Abraham
3.08 world
3.09 were very proud
3.010 are Jews
3.011 God
3.012 about Jesus
3.013 Jesus would be born
3.014 yes
3.015 no
3.016 yes
3.017 no
3.018 yes
3.019 yes
3.020 yes

LIFEPAC TEST

1. 3
2. 1
3. 2
4. 3
5. 1
6. 2
7. Babel
8. God
9. nations
10. Abraham
11. Israel
12. Jews
13. Hebrew
14. Jesus
15. Go
16. no
17. yes
18. yes
19. no
20. Go, teach, nations, I, always, end, world

ALTERNATE LIFEPAC TEST

1. no
2. no
3. no
4. yes
5. yes
6. yes
7. yes
8. Tower
9. heaven
10. language
11. task
12. love
13. Jews
14. a great nation
15. speak different languages
16. language became mixed up
17. name of Abraham's family
18. tell others about God
19. means *mixed up*
20. what people talk or write

BIBLE 209

ALTERNATE LIFEPAC TEST

Name _____

Date _____

My Score

16 / 20

Each answer = 1 point

Answer *yes* or *no*.

1. _____ The people wanted to build the great tower because they were humble.

2. _____ The tower was supposed to reach the highest mountain.

3. _____ The name of the tower was Bethel.

4. _____ God did not want the people to make their own way to heaven.

5. _____ Abraham's family became the nation of Israel.

6. _____ Jesus promised to be with us to the end of the world.

7. _____ The people forgot about God's powers.

Write the correct word on each line. Choose from the word list.

task	language	heaven	love	Tower

8.   The _____ of Babel was never finished.

9.   People wanted a great tower to reach to
       _____ .

10.   The people who first lived on the earth had only one
       _____ .

11.   To tell other people about God's love is our _____ .

12.   We will do what God asks us to do if we _____ him.

Draw a line under the correct answer.

13.   Jesus was born into the nation called the _____ .
       Gentiles

       Jews

       Philistines

14.   God promised Abraham _____ .
       a palace

       many languages

       a great nation

15. It is hard to tell people from other nations about Jesus because they _____ .

    live far away

    speak different languages

    wear funny clothes

16. The Tower of Babel was not finished because the

    _____ .

    people got tired

    people ran out of bricks

    language became mixed up

Draw lines to match the words.

17. Israel ▶   ◀ means *mixed up*

18. preach ▶   ◀ name of Abraham's
                         family

19. Babel ▶   ◀ what people talk or write

20. language ▶   ◀ tell others about God

BIBLE 210

Unit 10: God, His Word, and You

TEACHER NOTES

MATERIALS NEEDED FOR LIFEPAC	
Required	Suggested
(None)	• Bible

ADDITIONAL LEARNING ACTIVITIES

Section 1 - God Our Father

1. Discuss these questions with your class.

    a. Who put the love in parents' hearts that they have for their children?

    b. Does God love you as much as your parents love you?

    c. Does God love you more than your parents can love you?

    d. Why can your parents not love you as much as God loves you?

    e. Do you feel safe in God's love?

    f. What was the best way God showed His love for you?

2. Create a little drama.

    A number of children act like naughty or disagreeable children.
    Two children play the parts of parents who come in and show how loving parents deal with problems and discipline their children.
    All of the children discuss their ideas.

3. Draw pictures of things you can do to show kindness to someone else.

4. Make up a prayer of your own and write it in your best handwriting.

    Decorate the border.
    Paste it on heavier colored paper and hang it in your bedroom.

Section 2 - The Word of God

1. Review these Bible stories with your class.

    a. Daniel trusting God

    b. Moses, the leader

    c. David and Goliath

    d. Paul, the missionary

    e. the Creation

2. Make a mural of many of the things God created.

3. Write the psalm you wrote for Activity 2.16 (or another psalm) in your best handwriting.

    Decorate the border.
    Paste the psalm on colored construction paper.
    Perhaps you can hang it in the schoolroom or perhaps you will want to give it to your parents or a friend.

4. Make up a tune for the psalm you wrote (Activity 2.16). Sing it for the class or for your parents. Play it on the piano or another musical instrument if you can.

Section 3 - Life with God

1. Review with the class the events in the lives of these people:

    a. Joseph, b. Abraham, and c. Jesus.

2. Divide the class into two groups.

    The members of one group take turns saying something Jesus did. The members of the other group take turns saying whether or not we can do a similar thing.

Administer the LIFEPAC Test.

The test is to be administered in one session. Give no help except with directions.
Evaluate the tests and review areas where the students have done poorly.
Review the pages and activities that stress the concepts tested.
If necessary, administer the Alternate LIFEPAC Test.

ANSWER KEYS

SECTION 1

1.1	Jesus
1.2	God
1.3	Example: Because He made me
1.4	Jesus
1.5	Example: It makes me feel warm and safe and happy.
1.6	Drawings will vary
1.7	Drawings will vary
1.8	For God so loved the world, that he gave his only begotten Son, that whosoever believeth in him should not perish, but have everlasting life.
1.9	yes
1.10	no
1.11	yes
1.12	no
1.13	yes
1.14	yes

1.15

hat:	make:
happy	gave
glad	made
ask	say
bad	safe
sad	face
have	place

1.16

a. God	b. loved	c. he
d. only	e. Son	f. believeth
g. him	h. perish	i. everlasting
j. life		

1.17	Jesus
1.18	prayer
1.19	blessings
1.20	heaven
1.21	God
1.22	Lord's Prayer
1.23	talk
1.24	family
1.25	redeem
1.26	gifts
1.27	Son
1.28	above
1.29	won
1.30	live
1.31	rest
1.32	see

SELF TEST 1

1.01	yes
1.02	no
1.03	no
1.04	yes
1.05	yes
1.06	children
1.07	sins
1.08	heaven
1.09	blessings
1.010	faith
1.011	Jesus
1.012	home
1.013	gift
1.014	disobey
1.015	believe

SECTION 2

2.1	a. New Testament
	b. Old Testament
2.2	all things from creation until the birth of Jesus
2.3	the story of Jesus' life and the people who followed Him
2.4	books
2.5	many people who served God
2.6	no
2.7	yes
2.8	yes
2.9	no
2.10	no
2.11	a Spirit
2.12	a burning bush
2.13	Old Testament
2.14	God
2.15	were in Egypt
2.16	Example: I praise Thee, O Lord
	I sing to Thee
	Songs of thanksgiving
	I love Thee, O Lord
	I pray to Thee
	Prayers of thanksgiving

2.17

bed:	**he:**
pet	me
led	tree
get	see
fed	ye
met	we
ten	be

2.18	a. child b. known c. doings
2.19	missionary
2.20	New Testament
2.21	Jesus
2.22	Holy Bible
2.23	heart
2.24	Example:
	I can be kind and good.
	I can help my parents.
	I can tell others about God.
2.25	Example: I can show them my Bible. I can tell them how Jesus died for them. I can invite them to come to church.
2.26	no
2.27	yes
2.28	yes
2.29	no
2.30	yes

SELF TEST 2

2.01	in the Bible
2.02	no one (only Jesus)
2.03	to heaven
2.04	the burning bush
2.05	to praise God
2.06	yes
2.07	yes
2.08	yes
2.09	no
2.010	no
2.011	missionary
2.012	God
2.013	Son
2.014	Old Testament
2.015	God's plan
2.016	gift
2.017	sin
2.018	a. child b. known c. doings
2.019	a. God b. loved c. he
	d. Son e. believeth
	f. everlasting
2.020	talking with God

SECTION 3

3.1

live:	**light:**
give	right
with	fine
wind	smile
forgive	night
in	like
sin	kind

3.2   a. love   b. Lord   c. God
       d. heart   e. soul   f. mind
       g. commandment   h. love
       i. neighbour

3.3   Drawings will vary.

3.4   Example: I clean my room. I make my bed every day. I set the table for dinner and I take care of my little sister when my mother goes shopping.

3.5

love:	**told:**
from	fold
brother	home
some	below
above	goat
mother	roll
come	soul

3.6   Mary
3.7   God
3.8   God chose Mary
3.9   Mary's husband
3.10   an angel
3.11   Jesus
3.12   yes
3.13   yes
3.14   no
3.15   yes
3.16   yes

3.17

run:	**blue:**
sun	rule
fun	you
unto	fuel
up	clue
Jesus	suit
under	Sue

3.18   New Testament
3.19   Jesus rose from the dead
3.20   about the kingdom of God
3.21   in a manger
3.22   Example: I would hear Jesus teach the people about the kingdom of God. I would see Jesus heal sick people.

SELF TEST 3

3.01   Mary
3.02   gifts
3.03   heaven
3.04   Jesus
3.05   sin
3.06   Paul
3.07   Bible
3.08   yes
3.09   yes
3.010   yes
3.011   no
3.012   yes
3.013   yes
3.014   no
3.015   yes
3.016   yes
3.017   yes
3.018   no
3.019   no
3.020   Example: He rose from the dead and talked to his friends.
3.021   Example: To redeem us. To take our sins on himself.
3.022   Example: He taught people about the kingdom of God.
3.023   Example: You can read the story of Jesus, and stories about Moses, Daniel, and Paul.
3.024   Example: All people who love God and obey His Word.

LIFEPAC TEST

1. a Spirit
2. a burning bush.
3. God's voice
4. God's Son
5. in the lion's den.
6. pray to the king.
7. start churches
8. yes
9. yes
10. no
11. no
12. yes
13. yes
14. yes
15. no
16. created or loved
17. two
18. people
19. New
20. eat or bite
21. songs or psalms
22. Old
23. earth
24. Example: Because He made us and loves us.
25. Example: He died for us so that we could be God's children and live with him forever.

ALTERNATE LIFEPAC TEST

1. made
2. home
3. spirit
4. powerful, universe
5. prayer
6. faith
7. to disobey God
8. talking to God
9. more than enough
10. all of creation
11. to buy back
12. end of earthly life
13. a praise to God
14. something not understand
15. yes
16. no
17. yes
18. no
19. yes
20. yes
21. heavenly
22. Old
23. New
24. Example: Jesus died for us.
25. Example: We will go to heaven to be with God.

BIBLE 210

ALTERNATE LIFEPAC TEST

Name _____

Date _____

My Score

21
26

Each answer = 1 point

Write the correct word on each line. Choose from the word list.

universe	faith	made	prayer	powerful	home	spirit

1. We belong to God because He _____ us.

2. Because God cares for us He has prepared a wonderful _____ in heaven.

3. God is not a man but a(n) _____ .

4. God is very _____ because He created the _____ .

5. Talking with God is _____ .

6. Even though we cannot see God or always understand Him, we can have _____ .

Draw lines to match the words.

7. sin ▶   ◄ to buy back

8. prayer ▶   ◄ all of creation

9. abundant ▶   ◄ to disobey God

10. universe ▶   ◄ talking to God

11. redeem ▶   ◄ a praise to God

12. death ▶   ◄ more than enough

13. psalm ▶   ◄ something not understood

14. mystery ▶   ◄ end of earthly life

Answer yes or no.

15. _____ Moses saw a burning bush.

16. _____ Moses did not hear God's voice.

17. _____ Jesus is God's Son.

18. _____ Daniel was put in a den of snakes.

19. _____ Daniel would not pray to the king.

20. _____ Paul helped start churches.

Write the correct word on each line.

21. God is our _____ Father.

22. You can read about the Creation in the _____ Testament.

23. You can read about Jesus in the _____ Testament.

Answer these questions.

24.   What did Jesus do so that we could be God's children?

_____

_____

25.   If you belong to God, what will happen when you die?

_____

_____